Wake Up and Smell the Truth

Reverend David M. Berman

George Washington's
Thanksgiving Proclamation
In the year of our Lord 1789

WHEREAS it is the duty of all nations to acknowledge the providence of Almighty God, to obey His will, to be grateful for His benefits, and humbly to implore His protection and favor; and Whereas both Houses of Congress have, by their joint committee, requested me "to recommend to the people of the United States a DAY OF PUBLIC THANKSGIVING and PRAYER, to be observed by acknowledging with grateful hearts the many and signal favors of Almighty God, especially by affording them an opportunity peaceably to establish a form of government for their safety and happiness:"

NOW THEREFORE, I do recommend and assign THURSDAY, the TWENTY-SIXTH DAY of NOVEMBER next, to be devoted by the people of these States to the service of that great and glorious Being who is the beneficent author of all the good that was, that is, or that will be; that we may then all unite in rendering unto Him our sincere and humble thanks for His kind care and protection of the people of this country previous to their becoming a nation; — for the signal and manifold mercies and the favorable interpositions of His providence in the course and conclusion of the late war; — for the great degree of tranquility, union, and plenty which we have since enjoyed; — for the peaceable and rational manner in which we have been enabled to establish Constitutions of government for our safety and happiness, and particularly the national one now lately instituted; — for the civil and religious liberty with which we are blessed, and the means we have of acquiring and diffusing useful knowledge; — and, in general, for all the great and various favors which He has been pleased to confer upon us.

And also, that we may then unite in most humbly offering our prayers and supplications to the great Lord and Ruler of Nations and beseech Him to pardon our national and other transgressions; —to enable us all, whether in public or private stations, to perform our several and relative duties properly and punctually; —to render our National Government a blessing to all the people by constantly being a Government of wise, just, and constitutional laws, discreetly and faithfully executed and obeyed; —to protect and guide all sovereigns and nations (especially such as have shown kindness unto us); and to bless them with good governments, peace, and concord; —to promote the knowledge and practice of true religion and virtue, and the increase of science among them and us; —and, generally, to grant unto all mankind such a degree of temporal prosperity as He alone knows to be best.

GIVEN under my Hand, at the city of New York, the third
day of October, in the year of our Lord,
one thousand seven hundred and eighty-nine.
(signed) G. Washington

Contents

Foreword

Let me start by saying thank you for taking time to read this book. I have wanted to write this for a long time because of what I see as the deterioration of the founding principles of this great nation. As a minister I have counseled, prayed for, guided, and cried with many people over the years. Some of the problems people go through are simply because we live in an imperfect world. There are troubles like financial pressure, death, sickness, etc. On the other hand, many problems concerning relationships, finance, education, marriage, and morals are a direct result of a secularist worldview. Families struggle often because of how they look at life, and what principles they make decisions by. This book's purpose is to take a look at liberalism, truth, and how our national and cultural life has moved from a Judeo-Christian worldview to a secularist worldview. Just what are the consequences?

In this book I will touch some very controversial topics. These hot button issues always bring out emotions. In this book I have tried to make logical arguments so that people reading this will stop and think about their positions. It was also a consideration of mine to write this book in essay form so that everyone could clearly understand it. I, as a matter of choice, decided not to write a book with lofty terms. This is an easy book to read and contemplate. I trust that it will make you think.

Blessings!

Rev. David M. Berman

Acknowledgments

✦⟫═◉═⟪✦

*This book is dedicated to our founding fathers,
who gave it all for our liberty!*

*This book, and everything that I have accomplished in my life, is a testimony to my loving wife
Brenda who always stands by me. I want to also
acknowledge my children, Katherine, Heather,
Benjamin, Bethany, and Olivia,
who I love very much!*

*Special thanks to my brothers Arnie and Jerry,
who I love beyond words.*

*Special thanks to Janet Rua for her help in
editing and typing this book.*

A Basic Understanding of Worldview Influence

⊷⟫⟪⊶

To better understand the thoughts that shape cultures, it is helpful to look at the basic worldviews. This is not intended to give an exhaustive study of all worldviews, but rather to give an overview so the reader may gain more understanding of how basic thinking influences a culture. There are 4 basic worldviews from which religion is based on.

1) Monotheism
2) Polytheism
3) Pantheism
4) Atheism

These four words describe the basic views of philosophy.

1) Monotheism is the belief that there is one God, the Creator and Ruler of the Universe.
2) Polytheism is the belief that there are many

gods that rule the universe.

3) Pantheism is the belief that all things, and all life, are God, and part of the collective rule of the universe.

4) Atheism is the belief that there is no God, and that all there is in the universe is a result of natural means, with no creator at all.

In these four basic categories, there are very differing points of view. Clearly, one who holds to one of these beliefs will be quite different in worldview from one who holds to another. It is safe to say that any society that is based on a particular view will be greatly challenged at its core by the emergence of another worldview that is contrary. This is why our culture has fallen so far. We have left our founders' worldview. What we must decide as a nation is whether or not our founding principles are what made this country great, powerful, prosperous, and free.

Monotheism

Monotheism can be found as the basis for Judaism, Islam, and Christianity. The basic belief in one supreme God who rules the universe is the one thing each religion has in common. However, even while they share that one similarity, Islam teaches a very different view of God than Christianity, as you will see. Islam teaches of an impersonal God who must be served in a particular way in order to please him. A set of works that are known as the pillars of Islam is to be adhered to strictly. This view is also one of theocratic rule. Government must be Islamic. The Islamic worldview sees two worlds. One is made of those who are Muslim. The other is made of those who are not. The idea is to bring about submission to Islam by any means, including force. The five pillars of Islam for the individual are

1) **Faith**. This is called the "Shahada." It is to be recited and believed. The "Shahada" is recited as follows: "There is no God but Allah and Muhammad is His messenger."
2) **Prayer**. This is called "Salat." Obligatory prayers are to be said five times a day. They are to be said at dawn, noon, mid-afternoon, sunset, and nightfall.
3) **Giving**. This is called the "Zakat." This is compulsory giving to the poor and to the promotion of Islam.
4) **The fast**. This happens once a year in the

Muslim month of Ramadan. During this month fasting is expected between first light and sunset.

5) **Pilgrimage**. This is called the "Hajj." This pilgrimage to Mecca in Saudi Arabia is an obligation for those who are able physically and financially to do so.[1]

These "pillars" of Islam are to be done in order to work for salvation in pleasing God. This is what is known as a "works-based" religion to obtain salvation.

Polytheism

Mormonism is an example of polytheism. Mormons believe that God was once a man who earned Godhood, and in so doing gained this planet to rule over. They believe that they may also be able to attain Godhood through good works. They have a system of priesthood they use to bring them closer to their desire to obtain Godhood. Mormonism is another "works-based" salvation belief.

Pantheism

Hinduism, along with other eastern mysticism, is basically pantheistic. Followers believe in reincarnation, and desire to reach a higher plain of existence. In Hindu cultures, people are judged by worth based on a caste system. Reincarnation is seen not as a good thing, but rather as meaning that one's last life did not reach the place of dissolving into a sort of pantheistic god consciousness. Because of this worldview, those of lower caste are seen as being lesser in value. The lower caste is discriminated against in Hindu societies. One can see how discrimination is practiced on the basis of that worldview. If in a lower caste, one has not become as good as one in a higher caste. Hinduism is yet another "works-based" religion. It is not salvation they are working for in the Christian sense. Rather, followers look at salvation as getting to a place of non-existence - not an optimistic worldview at all. Hindu dominated cultures have been, for the most part, filled with poverty and despair. Such a worldview leaves its people without much optimism to prosper in this life.

Buddhism is another worldview that is extremely pessimistic. Buddhism holds to what is called the "eightfold path."

1) Right views
2) Right aspiration

3) Right speech
4) Right conduct
5) Right livelihood
6) Right effort
7) Right mindfulness
8) Right contemplation [2]

Buddhists believe in reincarnation. They see reincarnation as an endless cycle of suffering. The goal of the Buddhist is to break that cycle and reach "nirvana." Nirvana is defined as eternal nothingness. So what the Buddhist worldview is really about is ending one's own existence by extinguishing the flame of life. This view has certain implications to a society. Clearly it is pessimistic. In fact, Buddhists must work to convince themselves that they have no personal significance.

Atheism

Atheism is the belief that there is no supernatural life at all. It is the belief in nature and natural laws, with heavy emphasis on evolution thought concerning how life began. It is total reliance on mankind as savior of himself from all natural problems. Secular humanism is in itself a religion that puts its trust in the intellect, creativity, and experience of mankind.

This view has no thought of divine consequences for actions, and therefore has no basic code of principles, except what mankind determines is right and wrong.

It is clear from these examples, that there are different ways of looking at life. Basic worldviews influence the way a culture decides how it governs politically, and socially. Again, this is not an exhaustive study of world religion. It is instead meant to show how worldviews have an effect on society.

Christianity

The Christian worldview is quite different. The Christian sees the world as those who are Christian and those who are not. However, the Christian teaching is the conversion of the non-believer by a choice of his or her own free will. The Christian worldview is clearly a strong belief in God as personal and loving, and the belief that God rewards, in this life, those who walk according to his precepts. There is also what the Bible calls "blessed hope." This is a clear distinction of the Christian worldview. The Christian teaching about the position of man, and how man receives salvation is as follows:

1 All mankind is born in a sinful condition, and separate from God.

2) There is nothing a person can do to work himself or herself out of that sinful condition.

3) Because God is a God of righteousness, and justice, a price must be paid for sin.

4) God who is merciful became human flesh in the person of Jesus Christ and dwelt among mankind.

5) Jesus himself took the punishment for the sins of all mankind upon himself on the cross.

6) Jesus becomes personal (to the believer who accepts the free gift of salvation, provided by the sacrifice that Jesus made by taking the punishment for sin upon himself on the cross) through His Spirit, and brings a pardon from sin's consequence of separation from God.

7) Whosoever calls upon the name of Jesus, (Jesus is risen from the dead) and has their trust in his sacrifice for sin, is immediately saved from the wrath of God and becomes a temple of God's Spirit. This brings that individual into a personal relationship with God

Himself, and it frees him/her from the curse of sin and death.[3]

Christianity is "grace-based" religion, based on the work of God rather than the ability of man to save himself. Works are performed not to gain salvation but rather out of love for the Savior who paid the price for the believer.

Islam is very different from Christianity. In Islam, one never gains assurance that he or she has performed enough to gain eternal life. They live in fear of not making it to heaven. This is a pessimistic view of life and leads to forced conversion and usurpation of personal decision. Followers see a constant need to spread Islam by any means in order to please the Muslim God. In Christian thought, life is seen as a time to serve a loving God, and to prosper by His grace, with the promise of heaven to all who have received Christ as personal Savior. Clearly Hinduism is far from Christianity as well. Its view is similar concerning reaching a similar place as Buddhism in personal non-existence. Atheism leaves mankind with no moral absolutes at all. Communism is the great historical evidence of the failure of the atheistic worldview. It has been said: "religion has caused wars." That is true, however I must remind those who have said that of an important fact: Communist/Marxist (based on an atheistic worldview) governments have been responsible for the murder of an estimated 40 to 60 million people. Wars will always be a clash of worldview. Even with the liberal dream of one day having a utopian society, there never will be a united worldview until this world is over. Some believe in tyrannical leaders. Some believe in freedom. Some follow biblical principles, and some are relativists. To say that any society operates in a religious (worldview) void is not supported by study of any society.

It should be clear in looking at, for instance, the example of Islam vs. Christianity, that a society that is Islamic will have less freedom than a society that is Christian. The basic view of the world influences the governance of the society. Both the governing laws, and the social influences, will be much different in the example I have placed before you.

Christian belief is an assurance that brings an optimistic view of life. It brings peace, and a sense of desire to serve God rather than a law to do so. It is no accident that the Declaration of Independence, the Constitution, and the Bill of Rights are uniquely Judeo-Christian in their worldview. That is what has made America the free, optimistic, prosperous, powerful nation that it has been. It is impossible to separate a culture from its prevailing worldview. The two are one in the same. The prevailing worldview equals cultural practice. Because of the clear understanding of the Christian principles concerning one's choice to believe in Jesus Christ, freedom to practice other religions is protected by the First Amendment of the Constitution. Islam, for example, does not recognize this principle of choice to serve God. Therefore, Islamic culture sees no right to practice another religion. The point has been made that religion or worldview of a society determines the practices of that society in its governance, and culture. This truth is undeniable and has been proven throughout history.

One of the things that most disturbs me is the willingness of average people to accept illogical positions as truth. Over and over again the pop culture says absurd things and people just say, "Ok, it must be so." Pop psychology is one of the most destructive movements in our culture. So-called "self- help" books are all the rage. Interestingly, many of the "self-help" books do little more than foster a false position that makes one feel that they are a victim, and the center of the universe. The media, entertainment, and music industries, all motivated by political correctness, seem to be working in concert to undermine any common sense.

Religious Void

The biggest lie that is fostered in our modern society is the belief that any society can function in a religious void.[4] Many today try to make the argument that our founding fathers had a vision of absolute separation of religious principles from public society. One of those positions that I alluded to in the last paragraph is the notion that "you can't legislate morality."

I have heard people of the liberal persuasion preach that silly notion over and over. Let's examine that statement. If we legislate that murder is wrong and punishable, is that not a moral legislation? If we say that a corporate leader cooking the books is wrong, and punishable, is that not legislation of morality? Let me now take a favorite subject for the left. If we outlaw companies from releasing pollution, and we punish them for breaking the law, is that not a legislation of moral belief? Now the liberal might say, "Well we do not believe that absolute truth exists, we only believe in legislation that stops people from hurting someone else. But if it is not hurting anyone else, we should not legislate against it." That argument is clearly flawed. The position of saying that only things that "hurt another" should be outlawed is itself a moral judgment. Society is run by a set of moral judgments and there is no way around that!

The question is not *if* belief plays a role in societies' public policy, the question is *which* belief will play the role? I would argue that no one is without a religious philosophy (worldview). What is religion? It is a set of core beliefs that produce an action in the general life of the believer. If a person is an atheist, they still have a worldview. Theirs is a worldview that is called secular humanism. Secular humanism is the belief in humans as the deciders of what is right and wrong. It is really the worship of self-determining morals. That is in itself a religious belief. To the one who would say, "I believe there are no core beliefs," I would say that is clearly a religion of sorts (a worldview) and would fit the definition of a clear philosophy. The truth is that liberals are not really interested in separation of worldview from public society. They instead are quite interested in the replacement of the clear founding principles of the Judeo-Christian worldview, with a secular humanist belief based in pop psychology relativism. All is relative to them based on situation and the latest secular morals. They are so intolerant of the Judeo-Christian worldview that they will go to any lengths to remove our founding's influence on public society. They do this under the denial of historical fact, with the false assumption that our founding fathers had no relationship to Judeo-Christian principles in their writing of our founding documents.

The latest mantra is that "religion belongs in the home or places of worship only."[5] Do we realize what they are saying? They are saying that their ultimate goal is to remove the freedom of religious speech that is not in agreement with the secular humanist religion from the public arena. They have no problem with the teaching of new age philosophy, Native American religious philosophy, witchcraft earth worship, or any other philosophies that are in agreement with the secularist movement agenda. In other words, they really do not mind religion being taught or practiced in the public arena as long as it is not from the Judeo-Christian tradition. It's an alliance of sorts between secular humanists and non-Christian religious philosophy based on the desire to destroy our fundamental worldview. What is their agenda? It is anti-founding principles, anti-Bible, anti-Judeo-Christian tradition, and anti- Constitutional. I am blown away by how the left has used absurd interpretations of the Constitution to motivate activist judges to legislate the secular humanist agenda.

So the choice is ours as a nation. Do we want a set of core beliefs that have built the most prosperous nation in the history of mankind? Do we want the Judeo-Christian set of principles that has kept families together, crime low, teen pregnancy low, personal responsibility high, kids safe in school, and a generally prosperous society in family life, as well as finances? Or do we want the current situation? Crime high, teen pregnancy high, abortions high, education low, personal responsibility seemingly non-existent, kids afraid to go to failing schools, and a general breakdown in the family that is so severe that 70% of African American children, for example, are born out of wed-lock? I ask you to think.

In a country that spends so much money on education, one would think that the citizens should be clear on their understanding of our founding principles. Sadly, the education, media, and entertainment worlds have been substituting truth with blatant lies. The public has in many ways believed the lies, and propagated them as though they are fact. The basic worldview of any society will shape its social and public policy. We have been building some serious problems since we began to turn from our foundational Judeo-Christian worldview. What do we do about the destructive trends? The answer is obvious. We need to go back to our foundational principles. Yes, our nation was not perfect. Yes, we had issues that had to be addressed, but the principles that founded this nation gave us the tools to right those wrongs as we grew. By throwing our Judeo-Christian founding away and turning to the religion of secular humanism, we have strayed far from our founders' original intent, and from the worldview that so made us the envy of the world.

Truth:
The Founding Fathers' Thinking

⊷⇒⊜⇐⊷

The following is a speech I made at a 4ᵗʰ of July celebration.

We are living in quite a day right now and I don't have to tell you the effects that September eleventh had on our society. Some were immediate, but I think there are some effects that are long lasting. Who can hear "New York" and not think about what happened? Who can think about the Pentagon and not think of what happened? Who can think about Pennsylvania and not think about the plane that went down there? Who can think about freedom and not understand just how precious these things are to us?

Now I want you to know that the price of freedom is eternal vigilance. Up to now I think people have kind of taken it for granted. **Now some people may mock you or call you a flag waver, but I am proud to be an American. I will wave the flag and I don't care if anyone has anything to say**

about it. Do you understand? It represents something. "Oh that's old fashioned, that's this, that's that, you're a right-winger, you're one of those right wing religious rightists"...all these terms come out. I have yet to find somebody who can debate me on these issues who does not resort to these kinds of name-calling because the truth is on my side on these issues. We can just have a barbeque and talk about 'God Bless America' without understanding what it's all about. All the traditions of America: apple pie and Mom and baseball and all that stuff we love about the Fourth of July weekend. That's all wonderful, but you have to understand the reason we can do all these things is because some people paid with precious blood, a great price for your freedom.

The Fight Was For Liberty

The Revolutionary War was fought, really, by a rag-tag group of men who were fighting against a far superior military force. We knew that, but as the British were fighting for royalty, we were fighting for freedom. I have heard people say things like this: "Well, our military has fought for peace." Our military never fought for peace, our military fought for freedom. You can have peace under Communist rule, but that's not freedom. You can have no armed conflict under tyranny, that's not freedom either. They fought for freedom.

Self-Evident Truth

We all know these words, or we should, from the Declaration of Independence: "We hold these truths to be self-evident, that all men are endowed by their Creator with certain inalienable rights."[1] I want you to keep that in mind as we read Genesis 1:1. It is recorded this way in the first verse of Genesis chapter one: "In the beginning God created the heaven and the earth."[2] That's all the verse I want you to read. There is a truth there. Either God created the heavens and the earth or He did not. Either the Bible is true or it is not. Don't tell me, "well maybe some of it is a nice little story here and there." Either God created the heavens and the earth or he did not. He did not create half the heavens and earth. He did not kind of get the advice from some of the greatest scientists of man how to make the heavens and the earth. He did not ask Hollywood's opinion of what the heavens and the earth should look like. He created the heavens and the earth. This is the beginning of understanding the Judeo-Christian worldview. How do we look at the world? What glasses do we look through when we look at the world? "In the beginning God created the heavens and the earth."

Now go to John chapter three in the New Testament. Jesus says these words in John 3:21: "But he that does truth comes into the light, that his deeds may be manifest that they are done in God." Jesus mentions this word truth. In John 4:23 Jesus said, as He is speaking to the woman at the well about who He is, "But the hour comes and now has come when the true worshipers shall worship the Father in spirit and in truth." So the Bible says in verse twenty-one of chapter three that he who "does truth comes into the light, that his deeds may be manifest that they are done in God." Jesus said these words in verse twenty-three of chapter four "But the hour comes and now has come when the true worshipers shall worship the Father in spirit and in truth." Verse twenty-four says this: "God is a spirit and they that worship Him must worship Him in spirit and truth." Truth. Now the word is used, **and we have real fancy scholars out there who like to pick apart the Bible trying to find the original intent and meaning of the scripture, and that is certainly fine as we get into the original Greek terms,** but let me just tell you the word truth, beyond a shadow of a doubt, as you study intensely the original text, means truth. It's as simple as that. In fact if you study the original version of Genesis chapter one where it says "God created the heavens and the earth," in the Hebrew text it actually means: "In the beginning God created the heavens and the earth." This land was founded upon this truth. John 3:21 says "We do truth if we believe in God." If we trust the Lord according to His word. In verse twenty-three in John chapter four, it says we "must worship Him in spirit and truth."

John 14:6 says: "Jesus said unto them, I am the way, the truth, and the life. No man comes to the Father but by me." You cannot have it both ways. Jesus was not saying, "This is my truth, and you have your truth. You might have your truth but this is the truth I would like to give you at this particular time." Here is my truth: "I am the way, the truth, and the life." Do you realize the kind of statement He was saying? He was saying "I am the way, the truth, and the life. No man cometh to the Father but by me." Those are powerful words. If you do not believe He is who He said He is, you are calling Jesus a liar. I am about to ruffle your feathers and step on your toes. Some people get upset when I preach the Gospel; it's a good thing you do because I would hate to get no reaction. See, I want you to either bow your knee to Jesus Christ or I want you to get mad, but I don't want no reaction. That tells me you have nothing going on up there. I want some reaction that stirs your heart. My trust and hope is that if you do not make that commitment today, at least these words that I am telling you of what Jesus said will get into your heart and your mind.

In Genesis 1:1 it says: "In the beginning God created the heaven and the earth", John 3:21 says: "We do truth if we love God", John 4:23 says: "We must worship Him in spirit and truth," John 14:6 says He is "the way, the truth, and the life." Something else Jesus says in John 16:13, 14 when speaking of the **Holy Spirit was that Jesus would rise from the dead and after forty days ascend into heaven and then the Holy Spirit would be poured out upon the church. Speaking of the Holy Spirit He said**, "Now be it when he the spirit of truth is come he will guide you into all truth. For he shall not speak of himself but whatsoever you shall hear that he will speak and he will show you things to come. He shall glorify me for he shall receive mine and shall show it unto you." And so Jesus, when speaking about Himself speaks about truth, and when speaking about the Holy Spirit that he would guide you into truth. We are hearing a lot about truth today.

In the Declaration of Independence it starts out, "We hold these truths to be self-evident." When the Revolutionary War began and people left their homes to fight against tyranny, they were holding to these truths of life, liberty and the pursuit of happiness. In John 18:7 Pilate, the governing authority, confronts Jesus: "Pilate therefore said unto Him, 'are you a king then?' And Jesus answered, 'You say that I am a king, to this end was I born and to this cause came I into the world to bare witness to the **truth.** Everyone that is of the truth hears my voice." That's pretty cut and dry. He didn't say Buddha and I are the truth. He didn't say I, and in the future there will be a man named Mohammad, who is the truth. He didn't say the earth worshipper movement and I are the truth, Carl Marx philosophy and I are the truth, or the new age philosophy and I am the truth. He didn't say any of these things are the truth but Him. He said: **"I am the way, the truth, and the life. No man comes to the Father but by me."** Powerful words.

Modern Revision

You read in modern history books a revision of history that is unbelievable. No longer do we give any honor to our founding fathers, because of their flaws, and they had some flaws. I submit to you that our nation, which was founded on truth, began to be moved by that truth until the time when the Civil War happened and we had to right a wrong. It was inconsistent with the Declaration of Independence, "We hold these truths to be self-evident, that all men are endowed by their Creator with certain inalienable rights." We had to right that wrong, and it was done in the Civil War and blood was shed for it. We have had to right some other wrongs. But my friends, the foundation of this house that this nation was founded upon was the principles of the word of God, and the Lord began to deal with these various issues. "We hold these truths to be self-evident, that all men are endowed by their Creator with certain inalienable rights." Among those, the right to life. It is in the Declaration of Independence. People say, "Are you one of those crazy 'right to life' people?" Yeah, I am a crazy right to life person. I believe in a baby's right to life because the Declaration of Independence says, "We hold these truths to be self-evident, that all men are endowed by their Creator with certain inalienable rights. Among those rights are the right to life, to liberty, and the pursuit of happiness." Which in the context of those days clearly meant, **among other things, to be able to pursue dreams**, the ability to own property. Because in those days the elitists, the royalty, owned the property. You see, the Declaration of Independence was never meant to make us independent; it was really meant to transfer our dependence from worshiping some royalty across the sea that used its power for tyranny to a dependence on Almighty God, and to live in freedom under that dependence. This is the truth that has been lost in our school systems. They don't teach it any longer because it is not politically correct. Changing history to make someone feel good, stopping the valedictorian because you don't want to offend someone who may not be number one in the class, not keeping score when kids play sports: it's all craziness. Many of our schools, not all but many, it's been like a Carl Marx preschool and up through high school with socialism being taught, or Communism being taught. Someone's going to get upset because I'm talking about these things, but I'm in the business of bringing the message of Jesus Christ, of bringing the message of the Gospel, and if you read your

Bibles you will find there is no prophet in the Bible that someone didn't get mad at. Not one. My good Pastor friend said to me one day, "You need to be weary when all men speak well of thee, you have that one covered at least."

James Madison said this, and if you don't know who James Madison is then go to school and ask a teacher, and maybe they will know: **"We have staked the whole future of American civilization not upon the power of government, far from it. We have staked the whole future of all our political institutions on the capacity of man for self-government, on the capacity of each and all of us to govern ourselves, to sustain ourselves, according to the Ten Commandments of God."**

Truth vs. Relativism

There are basically two types of thought if you want to boil it all down. You have what is known as **thesis and antithesis** thought, which is the thought that there are absolute truth principles. Then you have what is referred to as **relativism**, where man determines truth due to the circumstance, or the political movement or the psychological movement of the day. So we have relativistic thought versus absolute thought. Make no mistake about it; our founding Fathers were absolute in their thoughts that God created the heavens and the earth, that we needed the permission of God to form this nation, and the blessing and protection of God to beat the enemy, which was holding our families in tyranny. They were not relativists who thought, well, tyranny is not true. Well, it might be your truth, but it's not my truth. The Declaration of Independence did not say "We hold these truths which are our truths to be self-evident to us, that at least in our truth we would like to be free but everybody else should not be free, or it would be nice if they were, but if you don't want to be free you don't have to be and if you want to hold someone in tyranny you can, because these are our truths." They didn't say that. They said, "We hold these truths to be self-evident, that all men are endowed by their Creator with certain inalienable rights." The word 'inalienable' means those rights cannot be taken away. Not justly anyway. That means man did not give us these rights, and man cannot take these rights away. The Supreme Court doesn't give us these rights, the Congressmen don't give us these rights, the Senate doesn't give us these rights, the President doesn't give us these rights, the bureaucrats don't give us these rights, and no one else gives us these rights. These rights come from God.

Do you understand how important it is to understand these truths? When you understand these truths you can sing these songs with understanding. But if you pick up any newspaper, or if you listen to the television today, you will find that it seems like nobody understands these truths. We have gone from true thinking to relativism, which says truth is based on what I think. Not absolute truth, but what you think it might be. "It might be your truth, it might be my truth, well that's good as long as you believe in something." Either God created the heavens and the earth, or He did not, and I am here to tell you that he did. Either Jesus is the way, the truth, and the life or He is not. And I am here to tell you that He is. This nation was built upon these truths, and all over they are trying to secularize everything. Anytime someone comes in mentioning God in the public square, they say: "Oh, you can't do that, the Constitution says so."[3] You had better read the Constitution. It never says you will stop people from exercising their religious faith. It simply makes it clear that the Congress shall not establish an official church. There will not be a Church of America, like there was a Church of England.

It is simple, and I submit to you that the reason this nation is great is not because of diversity, but because of truth and freedom. If people can thrive, can speak, can start businesses, can take a chance, can try to own some property, can better themselves by hard work, then it's freedom. It's freedom with the understanding that God governs us, we declared ourselves independent from the throne, and dependent on the true throne, which is God Himself.

Government & Christian Faith

On the relationship of government and the Christian faith, Psalms chapter two says, "Why do the heathen rage and the people imagine a vain thing? The kings of the earth set themselves and the rulers of the earth take council together against the Lord and against His anointed. They say 'Let us break their bands asunder and cast away their cords from us.' He that sits in heaven shall laugh and Lord shall have them in derision." Because God is God. The psalmist says that the kings set themselves against God; Hollywood can set itself against God, newspapers can set themselves against God, teachers and unions can set themselves against God if they want to. Churches that used to be churches and have a cross out front but don't know or teach about the Bible any longer, that have just become liberal social clubs for the advancement of socialism, can come against God if they want to, but God sits in heaven and laughs because He is God. He is able to defend himself, and in the final day He will. I read an article yesterday about how churches are very afraid to preach about hell now because they do not want to upset people. Well, guess what, there is a heaven to gain and a hell to shun. If that truth upsets you, then do something about it. Accept Jesus Christ as your savior, because He did all there is to do about it.

On the relationship of government and the Christian faith let me quote John Quincy Adams: **"The highest glory of the American Revolution was this, it connected in one indissoluble bond the principles of civil government with the principles of Christianity."** Daniel Webster said this: **"Our ancestors established their system of government on morality and religious sentiment. Moral habits, they believed, could not safely be entrusted to any other foundation than religious principal, not any government secure which is not supported by moral habits. Whatever makes men good Christians makes them good citizens."**

Benjamin Franklin said: **"Only a virtuous people are capable of freedom, as nations become corrupt and viscous they have more need of masters."** Daniel Webster also said: **"No government is respectable which is not just, without unspotted purity of public faith, without sacred public principle. Fidelity and honor no machinery of laws can give dignity to political society."** This is very interesting because we are told our founding fathers did not want any sense of God mentioned in schools or any other institution; we are told that to have a nativity may possibly cause harm to children. The Supreme Court said that if you post the Ten Commandments the children might actually obey them.[4] I wish I was making this stuff up; I wish it was not true that we have lost our mind as a nation. John Jay, the first chief justice of the Supreme Court, said this: **"Providence has given our people a choice of their rulers, and it is the duty, as well as privilege and interest of a Christian nation to select and prefer Christians for their rulers."** Now, whether you agree with his statement or not, let me tell you, don't revise history. John Jay said this. Here is another very interesting one. We are told that the First Amendment stops us from having religious freedom in school or in a public arena. Well interestingly, Fisher Ames, who earlier wrote the First Amendment, said these words: **"Should not the Bible regain a place it once held as a school book? Its morals are pure, its examples are captivating and noble, the Bible will justly remain the standard for language as well as of faith."** When you hear the lies and nonsense through the news media, you better come back to what your founding fathers said. That was their intention. **"The only foundation for a republic is to be laid in religion. Without this there can be no virtue, and without virtue no liberty, and liberty is the object and life of all republic governments,"** said Benjamin Rush, signer of the Declaration of Independence. Patrick Henry said: **"It can not be emphasized too strongly or too often that this great nation was founded not by religionists, but by Christians. Not on religions, but on the Gospel of Jesus Christ, for this very reason peoples of other faiths have been afforded asylum, prosperity and freedom to worship here."** Patrick Henry said it was built on the gospel. That's why we give the freedom to worship here for other religions, because their hearts must be changed by God and by the witness of the Gospel, not by the sword.

Self-Government

Our founders understood the way to be free was only in a society with a set of moral principles based on absolute truth. Self-government comes from personal commitment to God and His truth, which is the only truth. Apostle Paul said the church must be built upon truth, the pillar of truth, the only truth, and Jesus is called the only wise God. When people stop looking at God and His truth, they start moving toward relativism and slowly begin to call good evil and evil becomes good as deception comes in. They slowly move from truth and absolute truth and principles to relativism and thus they have the need for masters and ultimately look to government rather than to God. We are endowed by our Creator, not our government. Pretty soon truth doesn't matter and you don't know what the meaning of 'is' is. Because it doesn't matter, that's your definition.

I have heard people say this to me before, "You know, Pastor, you're narrow-minded. As long as you don't hurt anybody then there is no absolute truth." To which I say, well you said 'as long as you don't hurt anybody,' that's an absolute truth. Is there a problem here? You have to take it all the way. If you are saying to me there is no absolute truth as long as I don't hurt anybody, well who are you to tell me I can't hurt anybody? In fact if I punch you in the face right now, why can't I do that? I should have the right to do that if that's your philosophy, if that's your truth. I could punch you in the face right now and knock you out and it's not wrong. I decided it's not wrong because that's my truth. It might be your truth that it hurts and it is wrong, but it's not my truth and I feel fine. Do you understand the absurdity of that logic, or that lack there of? It's wrong for me to do it because it's wrong. Not because it's his truth or my truth, but because it's God's truth and God is true.

Endowed by Our Creator

We are endowed by a Creator, not by government. The more we slip from God the more people become unruly and have more need of masters. Our great founding father, Benjamin Franklin said that. He said you'd have more need for masters. George Washington, the great general and president with great insight said: **"Government is not reason, it is not eloquence, it is force. Like fire it is a dangerous servant and a fearful master."** James Madison said: **"I believe there are more instances**

of the abridgment of freedom of the people by gradual and silent encroachments of those who are in power than by violent and sudden usurpations." In other words, it's like putting a frog in a pot of water and turning the heat on. It begins to get hotter and hotter, slowly heating up until what that frog was is now dead. What's been happening in our nation is we have been slowly, slowly replacing the truth of life, liberty and the pursuit of happiness, of being one nation under God, to having our religious freedom abridged. Many in our country now want us to give sovereignty away. Many liberals are working to get us to submit to a court that is being set up by the United Nations to try our soldiers instead of having them under our laws, having them under our Constitution, our codes of military justice. They want to put us in some court run by world bureaucrats that are not elected by us. That is tyranny, and we must not have any of it.

We are in a time of war with blood being shed, our soldiers' and enemies' blood being shed; it is a very serious time to fight for freedom and the values of a nation. What values? You say we are here to defend our values. What are they? And who are we to say such a thing if it's not true? Why shouldn't they bomb the World Trade Center?

That's their truth. You see how absurd that thinking is? It's absurd. We are in this time of war, and in this time of war we have the **Ninth Circuit Court** saying that for kids to say the Pledge of Allegiance in school is unconstitutional because it mentions God.[5] And **I believe that the Supreme Court opens with some kind of prayer that goes something like 'God save the court.'** You know what's coming next: you can't sing God Bless America in school. You can't do that, it might offend somebody. Listen, it does not say in the Declaration of Independence: 'we hold these truths to be self-evident, that all men are endowed by their Creator with certain inalienable rights. Life, liberty and the pursuit of happiness and to never be offended.' It's not in there. Small segments of the population are atheist and are anti-Christ and anti-God and anti-America's founding, and the majority of the people have to suffer because of that. It's absurd.

Abraham Lincoln said: **"But for the Bible we could not know right from wrong. All things most desirable for men's welfare are found portrayed in it."** Right from wrong, perhaps that's why secularist society has denied the Bible, why they want nothing to do with the Bible. It is a book which speaks about how God is right and the Devil is wrong, and mankind has sinned, and sin must be dealt with, and it was dealt with by Jesus on the cross and we must accept Him as Lord and Savior and receive Him personally and believe and receive His sacrifice for us and go on to make some changes in the way we behave ourselves because there is a right and wrong. Secular society, which is relativistic, does not want any part of it. Abraham Lincoln said: **"If it was not for the Bible we would not know right from wrong."** Well my friends, Abraham Lincoln put his administration behind the war effort where the slaves were freed because there is a right and there is a wrong. Slavery is plain wrong! Had he the same mindset of so many today he would not have gone to war over that issue because it would have been their truth.

An American Patriot Holds These Truths

Our fathers shed blood for freedom, truths, and our rights. Our soldiers have shed blood for the protection of truth, and "we hold these truths to be self-evident." An American patriot is not someone who likes what they possess only, not someone who is only concerned with their own power like the elitists and the leftists are. A patriot of America holds these truths, that all men are created equal and endowed by their Creator with certain inalienable rights. You see, relativism does not allow you to hold these truths. If you are a relativist you cannot hold these truths, therefore you cannot believe what the Declaration of Independence says, and I am boldly going to say this: you cannot truly be an American patriot. Because a relativist cannot hold these truths to be self-evident. At best they can say well, I think this is my truth. Of what conviction are these great words of the Declaration of independence to a relativist? These words have no power to a relativist.

I am going to end with two more quotes, and these quotes could have been said by many today who would be called right-wingers, fundamentalists, crazy Christians, whatever they want to call it. They would have said: "Well maybe some crazy preacher said that, or maybe some intolerant conservative said that. Those guys are crazy; they would say that stuff." The first one is this: **"The basis of our Bill of Rights comes from the teachings we get from Exodus and Saint Matthew, from Isaiah and Saint Paul. I don't think we emphasize that enough these days, if we do not have the proper fundamental moral background we will finally end up with a government which**

does not believe in rights for anybody except the state." Any right-wing religious fanatic, according to liberals, could have said that. Any crazy bible preacher that gets up may say something like that, but I will have you know it was the thirty-third president, Harry Truman that said those words. How about these words: **"We have forgotten God, we have forgotten the gracious hand which preserved us in peace and multiplied and enriched and strengthened us. We have vainly imagined in the deceitfulness of our own hearts that all these blessings were produced by some superior wisdom and virtue of our own. Intoxicated with unbroken success we have become too self sufficient to feel the necessity of redeeming and preserving grace, too proud to pray to the God that made us.**" Unbelievable words. Did some right-wing crazy nut say them? No, Abraham Lincoln, in his Thanksgiving Proclamation, said them in 1863. Because these truths are self-evident.

When we celebrate our Independence Day we are celebrating truth. This nation was founded on Biblical principles. "One nation under God, indivisible, with liberty and justice for all." That is the goal. Are we a perfect nation? No, we are not because we are human. Do we have some injustice in our world?

Of course, we are human. The Bible tells us it is a sinful world. Not every American has bowed his knee to Jesus Christ, unfortunately. But it will be my job to preach the Gospel until every single person has come to Christ. And if you know Jesus it is your job to do the same. Because the truths that are self-evident are given by Him.

If you know Jesus Christ as your savior then you know truth because He is the way, the truth, and the life, and no man comes to the Father but by Him. Are you hearing me? Do you understand how important it is to pass these things on to our children? The predominant culture is not passing these things on. The predominant culture looks at every little mistake America ever made, puts down everything America ever did, puts down God and country. But I still believe in America, in apple pie, in faith, and in everything that is America because America is the land of the free and the home of the brave, as the song says.

Our men fight on that battlefield with a fire in their hearts because of these truths of freedom they are defending. They are worth fighting for, and we need to honor and celebrate our military. Let me tell you that we want to thank you from the bottom of our hearts for defending our freedom, defending our rights: life, liberty, and the pursuit of happiness. This is one nation under God, praise the Lord, amen.

Evolution vs. Creation

There is another very contentious debate taking place in our nation that has huge consequences. The debate has to do with the evolutionary worldview vs. the creationist worldview. My purpose in writing about this is not to spend an exhaustive amount of space defending my creationist view from a scientific argument. I could take this whole book and defend my position as a creationist from a scientific argument, however this book is about worldview. Most of my points will have to do with what the evolutionist worldview has done to our nation's conscience.

In times past we clearly had a worldview based on the Judeo-Christian perspective. (I speak about this in the essay on truth) What happens to a culture when it goes from believing in being created by the Creator, to the view of naturalism? If a nation has its basis in Judeo-Christian thinking, which clearly relies on the belief in creation by one creator who is super- natural, it cannot help but completely be turned upside down by changing to naturalism.

Naturalism

What is the worldview of naturalism? The naturalism worldview is that everything that we see, feel, smell, and experience is the result of a natural occurrence.[1] The naturalist believes that there is absolutely nothing supernatural. The belief in God is anathema to the naturalist. It is silly in their mind to believe in anything that one cannot observe. They believe that the Judeo-Christian worldview has its basis in superstition. Therefore, since in his or her mind there is no supernatural creator, there can be no supernatural moral law. Because there is no supernatural creator or supernatural moral law, mankind is free to create whatever moral or immoral society it chooses, based on mankind's own wisdom and experience.

Creationist View

The creationist worldview is that of cause and effect. Our belief is that this world could not have come from nothing. We believe that a creator made the universe, and that creator has shown us who he is in the evidence of his creation. The creationist believes that since the creator has made natural laws, it stands to reason that there are also certain spiritual and moral laws. Because of this, great emphasis is given to certain rights that are "self- evident."

This of course is the great battle that rages in our culture: the battle between the secularists and the traditionalists. As our nation has been teaching young people in the public schools the naturalist worldview, we have seen deterioration in the moral behavior of those who have grown up under its influence. One must ask the question that if there is no creator, who is to say what is right? This of course leads to situational ethics. Schools teach our young people that abortion is a choice and not murder. They teach sex is a choice, not a commitment in marriage. They clearly teach that there is no God to answer to. Why should any of those who believe in the naturalist viewpoint be shocked by the behavior of some young people today? In effect, the evolution/naturalist viewpoint has led to many cold-blooded crimes. The Columbine school shootings are a chilling example of what happens when people do not believe in the supernatural creator. The truth is hard to accept, however, I must say it. If your perspective is that there is no creator, no moral law, no judgment for evil behavior, and no absolutes in life, then a naturalist cannot label what happened at Columbine as wrong. The only way it could be labeled wrong is if there is a universal moral law that states it is wrong. The only way there can be a universal moral law is if there is a creator who made the universal moral law and expects His creation to obey it.

It is no accident that the Communists embraced evolution.[2] They saw it as perfectly fitted with their insane worldview. It is no secret that the Communists are responsible for the wholesale slaughter of millions of people. The Communist/evolution/naturalist view is what made it so easy to rationalize the killing of innocent people.

Radical Turn from Foundation

What Darwin did in his theory of evolution was to challenge the worldview that had prevailed in America. His theory is now taught as fact even though it has not, and cannot be proven. The evidence of evolution is filled with holes and totally absurd to try to defend. His philosophy has done more to destroy society that almost any other, because it attacks the core of social order. What he in effect taught is that there is no difference between mankind and any other animal.[3] Now when men and women behave like animals, people are shocked? Why should we be shocked? If there is no God, no moral law, no difference between animals and mankind, and no absolute truth, why should we not behave in a manner that is perceived best for the individual at the time? Why should an individual not kill another and take his food? Why should an individual not kill another who is old and in need of others to take care of him? Why should an individual share anything with anyone? Why should an individual have any moral compass at all? The clear answer of naturalism is an individual should behave like an animal to survive. Survival of the fittest is the key motivation of every living thing. Therefore humans are no different, and thus may do whatever is necessary to survive, even if that means murder.

I know some reading this will say that evolution is not meant to teach that. I must say however it can teach nothing else. Either God is the creator and naturalism is untrue, or this is all an accident and there are no moral absolutes at all. Some say that the only moral truth is that one's actions may not be allowed to hurt anyone else. The problem with that is the statement it- self is an absolute. Evolutionists cannot have it both ways. You cannot on one hand teach that all is the result of accidental nature, and at the same time say there is an absolute moral law. The two are opposed to each other.

Eyes Open Can See Design

Why is it that in the face of overwhelming evidence of a designer in the world's natural systems, that the establishment holds to evolution? It is extremely important to evolutionists that theirs is the only voice heard by our young people. They do not want any discussion of the possibility of a creator. They do not want both sides of the debate to be heard. Why? What are they afraid of? If the evidence for evolution is so sound, why do they not want kids to hear both sides and make up their own minds based on the evidence presented? If the belief in a creator is so silly, and there is no evidence to back up the conclusion that God does exist and did indeed create the universe, why would they not welcome the debate? It would be their chance to put away any doubts about their worldview.

Could it be that scientific discoveries like DNA evidence are making them nervous? Could it be that the truth of design found in DNA, as admitted by Professor Richard Dawkins, a highly respected Oxford evolutionist, is making those who have based their worldview on it scared? Dr. Dawkins wrote the following:

"After Watson and Crick, we know that genes themselves, with their minute internal structure, are long strings of pure digital information. What is more, they are truly digital, in the full and strong sense of computers and compact disks, not in the weak sense of the nervous system. The genetic code is not a binary code as in some telephone systems, but a quaternary code with four symbols. The machine code of the genes is uncannily computer-like. Apart from differences in jargon, the pages of a molecular-biology journal might be interchanged with those of a computer engineering journal."

Professor L.T. More of the University of Cincinnati said: "Our faith in the doctrine of evolution depends upon our reluctance to accept the antagonistic doctrine of special creation." He went on to say, "The reasonable view was to believe in spontaneous generation (evolution). The only alternative is to believe in a single, primary act of supernatural creation. There is no third position. For this reason many scientists a century ago chose to regard the belief in spontaneous generation (evolution) as a philosophical necessity." A PHILOSOPHICAL NECESSITY? Science is supposed to be an honest look at evidence, not a "philosophical necessity!"

Pride
Can it be that they have staked their reputations

on the "fact" of evolution? Can it be that if they admit the truth of creation that would mean that there could be absolute moral law? Could it be that there is no room for facts of evidence when they must protect their "philosophical necessity?" That is precisely the motivation of evolutionism/humanism/naturalism. This is precisely the reason why I say that atheism is a religion. Humanism is a religion, and naturalism is a religion. These are worldviews that are counter-productive to a free society that governs itself under divine moral law and restraint. Humanism brings more laws, not less, more centralized power, not less. History proves this fact in the example of the failed system of Communist/evolutionist/humanist societies like the Soviet Union, Cuba, and every other humanist culture.

We must not underestimate the power of human pride and arrogance. When one places their entire life in defense of evolution, and evidence continues to poke huge holes in their position, it is not easy for them to admit the truth. Pride and arrogance will stop even a scientist from seeing facts.

Clearly one of the most influential preachers of evolution was Aldus Huxley. He was a man so opposed to the biblical worldview, and the moral positions found in it, that he allowed his true motivations to come out concerning his promotion of the evolution theory. In the article "Confession of a Professed Atheist," Aldus Huxley is quoted as follows: "I had motives for not wanting the world to have meaning; consequently assumed it had none, and was able without any difficulty to find satisfying reasons for this assumption. For myself, as no doubt, for most of my contemporaries, the philosophy of meaninglessness was essentially an instrument of liberation. The liberation we desired was simultaneous liberation from a certain political and economic system, and liberation from a certain system of morality. We objected to the morality because it interfered with our sexual freedom."

What a remarkable admission of the true motivation of early evolutionists. The motive is not science. It is not the quest for observable truth. It is not the quest for objective evidence. It is instead a convenient way to deceive oneself into not having to answer to God! Evolution is the faith of the Atheist. The naturalist/humanist connection cannot be denied.

The Real Motive

In the Atheist publication "Humanist Magazine"

Professor J. Dunphy wrote an article entitled "A Religion for a New Age," and I quote: "I am convinced that the battle for humankind's future must be waged and won in the public school classroom by teachers who correctly perceive their role as the proselytizers of a new faith: a religion of humanity that recognizes and respects the spark of what theologians call divinity in every human being. These teachers must embody the same selfless dedication of the most rabid fundamentalist preachers, for they will be ministers of another sort, utilizing a classroom instead of a pulpit to convey humanist values in whatever subject they teach, regardless of the educational level. Preschool daycare or large state university. The classroom must and will become an arena of conflict between old and new - the rotting corpse of Christianity, together with all its adjacent evils and misery, and the new faith of humanism. It will undoubtedly be a long, arduous, painful struggle replete with much sorrow and many tears, but humanism will emerge triumphant. It must if the family of humankind is to survive."

This telling statement is clearly revealing the motivation for keeping creationism out, and making children swallow evolution as fact. The only thing that is "rotting" is the moral fiber of our culture. Christianity is not rotting; it is the only life-line we have to sanity in our social order of freedom. The more we embrace evolution/naturalism/humanism, the more we rot from within. There simply is no defense for not allowing the creationist point of view in the debate. There is in fact an agenda. The agenda is to remove any thread of the Judeo-Christian worldview from our society.

What Happened To the Church?

When one drives through any old New England town there is one thing you always see: a church at the center of the town. The cradle of our founding as a nation is New England. Today most of New England has left its roots. Most of the northeast of America is very liberal and in many ways hostile toward believers in Christ. The church is the place where the community used to gather for spiritual instruction from the Bible. It was also the center of social life.

Bad Seed

As the years went by the introduction of liberal theology entered into many seminaries. It used to be that the seminary was a place to learn of the power of God, and his word. Seminary was a place that welcomed thesis and anti-thesis thought. The liberal theology that crept into the seminaries, and the many colleges that were founded on Christian principles, questioned the original biblical faith. An outright war has been raging against the Bible. This assault on the Bible started in the middle of the nineteenth century. It intensified more toward the end of the nineteenth century, and really started to take hold into the twentieth century.

The Birth of the Bad Seed

Fast forward to the nineteen sixties, and you see a huge increase in the effects of the liberal theological mindset. It was like all the seeds of liberal thought were birthed in the sixties. The mainline churches began to give in to the pressure of liberal thinking. The pop culture began to embrace the liberal viewpoints of the sixties generation. College campuses became the breeding grounds for every leftist point of view. Many universities that were founded on biblical principles turned from their roots to liberalism. Harvard, Princeton, and many others became more like secularists than believers. All of this has had a dismal effect on many churches. Churches made decisions not to deal with heresy. Churches made decisions to look the other way when it came to dealing with outright rebellious behavior of professors and clergy.

The churches I mentioned in the center of towns used to be filled with biblical preaching. Clear standards of behavior were in place. Social relationships helped to keep families strong and committed. What happened to the church? Along with the decay of seminaries came the decay of the churches in America. Churches began to believe that they had to give in to pop culture pressure or members would leave. Liberalism took over and we now have many mainline denominations that hardly resemble the powerful churches of the past. Telling information was revealed in a Barna research study, reported by World magazine in 2004. The study concluded that less than half of all "Christian" ministers have a basic biblical worldview. The study showed that of the least likely to have a biblical worldview were seminary graduates. The word "Christian" is thrown around and used to describe any building with a cross on it. There are many buildings with crosses on them that have no resemblance to anything Christian at all. To be Christian is to believe what Jesus said. To be Christian is to believe the Bible, and to hold to it in the midst of pressure to pull back. Is it any wonder why the liberal churches have become little more than liberal, leftist social clubs?

The Effects of Bad Seed

The American society is now mostly illiterate

concerning biblical teaching. The average person gets their biblical knowledge from places like old movies, or the history channel.[1] The average person believes that statements like "God helps those who help themselves" are a Bible verse. It is not a Bible verse. Most people in America today do not understand the reason that Jesus died on the cross. They do not know about the fact of sin, and that Jesus took sin upon himself for us so that we may be saved if we trust in him. Even many who sit in churches on Sunday mornings are biblically illiterate. The average Bible reading of people who say they are church attending Christians is very low. The world calls out for relevance, and the answer is clearly told in the Bible. What is the problem? The problem is that many churches have bought the lie that says people are not interested in learning the Bible. In many mainline churches the Bible is not even spoken of. The Judeo-Christian worldview is not lifted up as the desire. Liberalism has replaced the word of God in many churches in America. I can say from my own experience that people are very interested in the Bible when the teaching of it challenges them. Real and serious Bible preaching moves people to decisions about life.

When I speak of liberalism I am speaking really

of the leftist agenda. I am not speaking of church style. I am not speaking about the use of hymns or modern style of music. I am not speaking about whether a service is liturgical or less structured. I am speaking about the core belief and worldview of the church. The liberal churches are churches in name only. They have left the Bible and in many ways have contributed to the decline of our nation much more than any atheist has. This society, having been founded on biblical principles, relied on the church to be the protector of those principles. As the churches became liberal in their thinking they began to stop holding the founding principles in high esteem. That has lead to not only a decline in the foundation of this nation, but also the decline in church attendance. The giving in to pop culture for the sake of not offending members has backfired. Many liberal mainline denominations have seen their attendance decline drastically. They have become irrelevant.

The churches that have grown have been those who preach the Bible. These churches have become relevant to the needs of society not by caving in, but rather by providing answers. By giving solid principles to stand on, Bible-believing churches bring needed stability to families and individuals. Our pop culture society today looks at preachers of the Bible with contempt. Pastors are often portrayed in Hollywood in very negative ways. Clearly, gospel ministers are not held in high esteem by the prevailing culture.

Religious Political Correctness

How have most churches responded to the decline of our nation? The response has been to cave in on many issues. The response has been to allow political correctness to drive the debate. Even Bible churches are compromising more and more on stances that are not politically correct. The road will lead to the same place as the mainline churches in the past have gotten to. The church must reject Liberalism! The only institution that has the power to save this nation is the biblical church. The clear principles in the Bible are what made this nation great, and are what will save it. The fact is that most preachers today are afraid. They are afraid of their own church boards. They are afraid they will get fired, or not asked to become a church's pastor in the first place. The sad lack of guts in the ministry today is disheartening. Instead of being leaders of the flock, many pastors follow the status quo. This means there are many pastors who believe the Bible but are not effective in spreading the truth of our founding biblical principles.

Let me say this clearly: I am not saying all churches are like this. I am not saying there are no good churches that take the heat and stand for Judeo-Christian principles. I am saying that there are far less than there used to be, and the latest information is not encouraging. The pastors in this nation must decide whom they work for. If a pastor thinks he works for the church then the pastor will not lead or be bold. However, if a pastor realizes that he works for God, he will preach and act upon biblical truth. <u>A PASTOR WHO UNDERSTANDS THAT HE WORKS FOR GOD WILL NOT BE AFRAID OF LOSING HIS POSITION!!!</u> He will preach the Bible and look at people without fear in his eyes. He will speak not only in the confines of the church walls, but he will also go into society and deliver the message of biblical principle. He will stand for pro-life, pro-family, and stand against the anti-Christ positions of the left. **A pastor who knows his leader is God will proclaim the gospel truth with fire in his bones, passion in his voice, and power in his example.**

The Only Answer

The time has come for Bible-believing preachers to go forth with confidence in the power of biblical principle. Preachers must stop checking their sermons with the thought police of the politically correct pew sitters. It simply makes no difference what the elitists think about what a true preacher speaks. If I may be bold, let me also say it makes no difference what church members think about the Bible being preached. Preachers are under no obligation to be pleasing to the ears of their followers. The fact is that preachers must be willing to lose their position if necessary rather than compromise on the Bible. Preachers of the Bible are under one obligation, that is to preach the Bible, and challenge all who hear their voice to respond to God's word with an amen. Too many pastors today have deceived themselves into thinking that they must not offend anyone. They are afraid to make waves, and are afraid to be called names.

We are in a serious culture war. This war is for the soul of our nation. We have been sleeping at the wheel while our country turns more and more to leftist, socialist policies. The church in many ways has been arguing about style of ministry, and unwilling to take a stand on issues of substance.

Parental rights are being stripped. We have conferences and meetings. We have books, tapes, and every kind of media about church growth. We have technology that surpasses our wildest dreams. We have radio and TV shows with grand-looking props. Even with all of this, we are missing some essential ingredients needed for revival in this land. Those ingredients are:

1) The absolute truth found in the Holy Bible.
2) The guts to take a stand on that absolute truth regardless of the cost.
3) The willingness to lose some people in our congregation if necessary.
4) The commitment to lead rather than follow.
5) The willingness to put our money where our mouths are by supporting the work of God's men.
6) The willingness to have our character assassinated by liberals.
7) The desire to see that all people that we come in contact with come to the understanding that Jesus is Lord. He is the Savior for all mankind. The desire to have everyone we meet understand what Jesus said of himself, and I quote: "I am the way, the truth

and the life, no man comes to the father, but by me". That by their own free will they may experience the only truth there is!

The family is under serious attack, and the powers that be are doing their best to remove all historical reminders of our Judeo-Christian heritage. What have the churches been doing about it? The answer is not much. We have not been influencing our culture like we once did and we cannot blame anyone else for that. We must have revival in our churches, and that comes from a respect for God's absolute truth. Revival will not come from another book or church growth seminar. It will come from turning back to truth, and from preachers who are not afraid to preach with power!

No one likes to be called names. No one likes to offend people, and be looked at in a negative way. Having said that, preachers must understand that they are not in a popularity contest, and it is not a political position.

I speak as one who understands personally the pain of having lies told about me. Many accusations are thrown my way because I take a biblical stand on issues. I understand because I have been preaching the Gospel since 1985. I have lost church members at times because they did not like what I said from the church pulpit. I must say that I am sure that many of my own fellow ministers will even attack me for what I am writing in this book. I have been called every bad name you can imagine. I have been called a "woman hater" because I stand against abortion. I have been accused of not caring about the poor because I am against the socialist policies of the left. I have been called a hater because I have stood for traditional marriage. I have been called harsh even by my own profession because I believe God's word, and I say what I mean, and mean what I say. It is unfortunate that many Christians think it is harsh to stand for clear biblical truth. The funny thing is, much of the time the lies and charges have been leveled at me by so-called "tolerant, enlightened, free speech, peace-loving" liberals. The not so funny thing is that way too often the lies and charges have been thrown at me by people who claim to believe the Bible but have no guts to stand up for it's truth. It has been Christians who are unwilling to take the heat, who have watered down the teachings of the Bible. In no other area have they watered down the Bible like they have concerning the family structure and order. Feminist, liberal, anti-authority "Christians" have given in to and often herald the modern politi-cal correctness that plagues this postmodern society we live in.

There is only one answer for the church. It is the same answer that God has given his people over and over in the Bible. The answer is found in the book of 2 Chronicles 7:14, **"If my people, who are called by my name, will humble themselves and pray and seek my face and turn from their wicked ways, then I will hear from heaven and will forgive their sin and will heal their land."** Who are we to believe that we have the right to call ourselves the church and not hold the sacred scrip-tures in the highest esteem? I am not speaking of any of us being perfect. I am speaking of us not holding up the perfect word of God as the goal. The church must get back to its place as the provider of truth and stop being influenced in the doctrines of the world's vain philosophies. Jeremiah, the great Hebrew prophet, said in Jeremiah 17: 5-6: "The Lord says cursed is the one that trusts in man, who depends on flesh for his strength and whose heart turns from the Lord. He will be like a bush in the wastelands; he will not see prosperity when it comes. He will dwell in the parched places of the desert, in a salt land where no one lives."

We may have money, but we have lost the prosperity in our families, our churches, our society, and our relationships because we have forsaken the Bible and have replaced it with psychology, liberal thinking, and political correctness. May our hearts be turned back to God's word, and may that begin with the preachers receiving again God's vision and boldness so that the church will again be an influencer, instead of an influencee. Amen!

The Emasculation of Males & Breakdown of the Family

O ne must only turn on the TV to see the continued assault on the American male.[1] Over and over, sitcom after sitcom, the portrayal of men is consistent. Men in the home are portrayed as stupid, bumbling idiots, incapable of making decisions, and simply out of touch with any ability to lead. Yes, I said the word that makes so many upset today: "lead." Yes leadership in the home is out of the question today for men in our politically correct culture. The mere mention of a man being a leader in the home evokes the worst criticism and name calling by the established secularists. Those who have swallowed hook, line, and sinker the secularist view lash out at those who hold the Judeo-Christian worldview. Facts do not seem to matter to those emotional secularists who preach the false gospel of secular humanism.

Men & Women Different?
A few years ago a major magazine had on its

cover the incredible finding that "men and women may be different."[2] Maybe it's me, but it seems like that is common knowledge. I am not speaking about the obvious differences. Anyone who has any doubt about the emotional differences should talk to me. I have 5 children, one boy and four girls. I know the differences in the way males and females tend to think and behave. I have been a pastor for many years and have counseled numerous couples. I can tell you that men and women are different in the way they think, and the needs they have. This should be common sense. The feminists have tried hard to make us all believe that the differences are because of societal pressure. They point their fingers at the culture and say that women have been kept back from success because of a male-dominated society. Are women really happier today? Are women really more fulfilled today with the breakdown of the family, and with few men that are willing to lead and treat them special like a man should? Are women really happy today with a culture that now teaches men to be irresponsible to their families? Are women more satisfied now with the primary responsibility of raising their children themselves? All my years of ministry, and all the counseling I have done, tells me women are not more fulfilled today. I see the results of our pop culture. I hear the pain in the hearts of women who cannot understand why they have been let down by men in their lives: men who were not responsible to take care of their provisional and emotional needs, men who were unwilling to commit to them in marriage, and men who wanted sexual relations with no emotional commitment to them at all. What the secularists and the feminists fail to see is that the feminine qualities of a woman are what make a woman who she is. True fulfillment is found in embracing the qualities that our Creator gave us. The hormonal make-up of a female makes her unique. A male is what he is because of his hormonal make-up. Our Creator gives these traits to us. He made men to be men, and women to be women. So many women have been hurt today not by the traditional movement, but rather by the result of secularist philosophy that has all but destroyed the family. The role of father and mother brings a great balance to children. They can experience the feminine soft qualities and the male qualities of provider and protector.

At What Price?

Why does this offend so many liberal women? I

believe it is insecurity. They have believed the lie that softer means weaker. They have believed that different means not as good. This issue of men and women is one of order and not one of worth. I cannot think of a more difficult and important role than that of nurturing mother. The worth of that goes far beyond her children but also to generations after. The same can be said for men. Men who properly lead and protect their family bring a sense of security to the family that only they can. They teach their boys to love their wife and provide for their children when they grow up and become husbands and fathers. They teach girls what kind of man they should look for when they are ready to marry. Now for those who are now offended because they are single parents or were raised in a single parent family, let me ask you a question: should we be striving for the best situation? Or should we not strive for the best situation because some who are not in the best situation will be offended? The answer is obvious. We should lift up as the goal in anything, what we know to be the best. The home with a father and mother in a loving relationship and order is by far the best goal. We as a nation should have policies that support and encourage that goal. We should stop pretending that men and women are the same and instead embrace the great complimentary differences. If we take an honest look at the results of the last 40 years we can only come to one conclusion: the majority of the feminist movement is a dismal failure. Oh yes, women are earning more money, having careers, and involved with many things. I must however ask another question: at what cost? The magazines glorify the "free lifestyle" of liberated women. These ideas also send a very clear message to men. The message is that women are no different. The question then becomes: why should I treat a woman different? What obligation do I have to a woman? They can fend for themselves. If we teach boys that there is no difference between them and girls, then why are we so surprised to find out that when those boys become men, they have no regard for their responsibility to lead, protect, and provide? The signal has been sent for 40 years and we are suffering because of it as a society; two parents working while the kids are neglected of the love and time they need. Worse than that is the amount of single parents that are working so much that they have almost no time with their children. Many children are being raised with little or no influence from their own parents. Clearly, men function best when challenged to lead, protect, and provide, and women function best when their feminine qualities are embraced and encouraged. In the roles that God has established for us we see harmony and blessing. In the roles that we have decided are better than God's design, we have seen terrible emotional, financial, and relational dysfunction.

Can anyone really say that there has not been a detrimental effect on children? Do we not understand that children need two parents? Whenever I talk about this subject, I always find that some people get offended. A single mother for example may feel that I am being unfair. I think it is important to look at the best scenario as the goal. I am well aware that at times, situations and circumstances may be such that the best is not attainable. Having said that, I still believe we should not lower what we know to be the best scenario as the goal. It is beyond a shadow of a doubt to any thinking person, that a father and mother raising children with love is the single best scenario for children to be raised in. The traditional family structure brings all the components necessary to the child to learn a healthy lifestyle. A boy learns how to be a man, and what qualities to look for when he is old enough to look for a wife. A girl learns how to be a woman, and what qualities to look for when she is ready to find a husband.

God Calls Men to Love

The radical feminists speak as though males are inherently looking to hurt and abuse their wives.[3] They act as though traditional Christian teaching is instruction to men on how to be mean to women. Let me set that straight. In the New Testament book of Ephesians, chapter five, the Apostle Paul clearly teaches: "Husbands love your wife as Christ loved the Church." The husband is seen as a representative of Jesus in the home. The Bible is clear concerning God's desire that men love their wives. When we read further in chapter five we see that Paul teaches: "He who loves his wife, loves himself." No man is ever given the right to be mean, unkind, or abusive to his wife in the Bible. No woman is ever given the right to be mean or rebellious to her husband either. The Bible instead instructs a man to lead his family in love, and to work hard to provide for his wife. He is instructed to be the spiritual leader of his whole household as well. If some men have twisted the Bible as a way of justifying abuse then they have done just that: twisted it. Some women feel that the fact that some men have abused their position gives them the right to ignore the teaching of God's word. That is not the case. That is like saying that if one police officer abuses his authority, that gives us the right to ignore the authority of all police. Individuals who abuse their authority should be dealt with individually. We must not blame all for the abuse of some. The radical feminists have used their disdain for any leadership position of the man in the family to misrepresent that which the Bible actually teaches. There is great security emotionally and spiritually, when the man leads his home as the Bible teaches. I will not step back from that truth, knowing full well that I will be maligned for speaking it. Let me say it clearly: God has established that the man is the head of the home, and when a man leads as the Bible teaches, and the woman operates in her role, the power of God's blessing is awesome!

Oh...What a Price Has Been Paid

The clear facts are that the family is suffering in every way since the secularists have gained control of the media, education, and entertainment world.[4] Marriage is no longer seen as important before having children. Divorce has skyrocketed. Little girls are encouraged to dress like streetwalkers, and boys are not taught their important role as leader, provider, and protector anymore. School violence has been attributed to not enough opportunity for kids, and not enough money being spent on education, etc. The problem is simple. The family is being torn apart by policies and philosophy that have been a proven failure. Why is it that so many children are raised now without a father in the home? Why is it that the sense of responsibility for one's own children seems to be lacking? Why is it that an increase in financial problems exists in the family? Can the answer be that the secular mindset has caused much of the woes? <u>Oh, it can not even be considered that the secularists who ban the Ten Commandments, cry separation of church and state at any mention of God, and cry free speech unless the speech is not politically correct, could be at fault.</u> Well let me say it clearly, and in terms that may upset the pop culture secularist types. The secular views that have so emasculated men, substituted psychology for biblical understanding, encouraged irresponsibility, and taught that government and more money are the answers to the social problems we suffer: **THEY AND THEIR PHILOSOPHY ARE THE PROBLEM!**

What we desperately need in our society is a

return to God, the Bible, church, and an under-standing of the Judeo-Christian principles that made our country what it once was. Those principles kept families together. Even though our country has never been perfect, we have been the envy of the world. Money is not the answer, taxes are not the answer, psychology is not the answer; God is the answer! A dependence on the principles of our heritage is the answer! A rejection of the postmodern mindset and secularist dogma is a must if we are to survive as the nation that we once were!

We must have pastors who are willing to take the heat from a culture that holds men of God in contempt. In my view, the country would change almost overnight if ministers would preach as they once did in this nation.

We now have half of our "Christian" ministers in this country that no longer hold to a biblical worldview. Is it any wonder that we have fallen so far? When the ones who are called to give us a moral compass are lost themselves, it becomes the blind leading the blind. Where are the men in this country? Where are the men who are willing to stand up for truth in the face of the secularist opposition? Where are the men who will stand and protect the founding principles of this great nation?

Disrespect of Christian Women

What about the women who believe in the Judeo-Christian principles of our founding? Why does the liberal establishment not hear them? Whenever there is a question about "women's issues," whom does the press go to for comment? The National Organization of Women. The fact that there is a bigger organization called Concerned Women for America is irrelevant to the press. The press all but ignores them even though they have more members than the left wing National Organization of Women. Why? Because the Concerned Women for America is a conservative organization. The secularists cannot allow any conservative women to be heard. The clear bias in the media, educational system, and entertainment world is painfully obvious.

For those of you who read this and have the typical liberal reaction, let me assure you that I am not advocating that we force anyone to adopt a particular religion. I am however using my free speech to hopefully get you to rethink what the politically correct crowd has preached. I am simply saying that our culture is decaying at a rapid rate, and the answer to the problem is only found in the people of America turning away from the foolishness that we have bought into. We must as a nation of individuals turn back to our founding by our own free will. May God bring us to that understanding before it is too late.

Marriage

The discussion of social topics in America over the last forty years has turned into an assault on all things traditional. Social policy has largely been influenced by what I would call "social engineers". Most of the social engineers do their theoretical papers, social experiments, and policy recommendations with a clear desire to make a change in society. This change is based on a secular humanist view of the world. They use lofty terms, fancy brochures, and whatever strange new words they can come up with to influence the culture. We have put such trust in them as a society. The pure psychobabble is mind-boggling. The redefinition of every institution that has made this country great is the goal of the social engineers. Their actions can only lead to one conclusion. That conclusion is this: they have a clear and obvious disdain for the traditions of this land!

This land has been the envy of the world, and the desire of many around the world has been to come to America. Why is it that we have prospered? Why is it that our crime rate in the past has been relatively low? Why is it that our economy has been so strong over the history of our nation? Even though there have been times of economic stress, our nation's history is filled with prosperity.

Social Engineering

Social engineering and new philosophy have had an impact on every institution in our nation. I would argue that one would have to be completely void of reality if not able to see the detrimental effects of the secularist influences. No other institution speaks this argument more than the institution of marriage. Marriage once was lifted up as the desire of most, the place where a male assumed responsibility concerning provision and the place where the female assumed the responsibility of nurture. This powerful combination led to stability in the home and thus in society. Now I must say that the picture was not rosy in every home. Because we are all sinners who need the Savior, it is clear that some homes were not happy. Having said that, it is also clear that there are a whole lot more unhappy homes today then there were then. The results of all the social engineering in the home have been a colossal failure. Every social problem including education weakness, crime, domestic violence, poverty, depression, poor health, lack of respect for authority, teen pregnancy, sexually transmitted diseases, abortion, etc., are a direct result of the breakdown of the family. The end of marital commitment causes the breakdown of the family. This lack of commitment has led to children being in the home without a father. The social engineers, along with the feminists, have been preaching that the father is really not that important. In fact, many in the lesbian movement feel that all they need is a sperm donor for conception, and after that the man is really not needed. Let me state some disturbing statistics.

1) Thirty-one percent of children now live without two parents in the home.
2) Twenty-two percent of children live with their mother.
3) Four percent of children live with their father.
4) Four percent of children live with neither their mother nor father.
5) Thirty-three percent of all births now are to unmarried women.
6) Two-thirds of the women under the age of twenty-five who are having babies are not married.[1]

The idea today is that there are "many types of families", and that no family structure is inherently better than the next. Single parents, cohabitation with no commitment, and any other way a person chooses to structure what they perceive as a family, is acceptable. In fact the liberals feel that any family structure is fine for children.

The Homosexual Agenda

With a clear anti Judeo-Christian secularist mindset, the gay and lesbian political agenda pushes for, and even promotes as desirable, so-called "gay couples" or "gay families" adopting children.[2] They feel the need of both sexes in the life of a child is outdated religious absurdity. For them, their philosophy is not in keeping with the Judeo-Christian worldview. The need for both male and female influence in a child's life is ridiculed by those who really are self-centered, and unwilling to put the needs of the child above their own unnatural sexual desires. Their attitude is: "this is what I am and it will be accepted". It makes no difference what every study shows about the need of children to have the traditional one-man, one-woman marriage-based family. Those who have the "me agenda" are unwilling to see the truth because they are blinded by the lust of self-desire.

The issue of the definition of marriage is one of the most ridiculous arguments we have ever had. Who would have even considered that we would have to discuss the definition of marriage? It is like discussing the definition of water. Water is water, and marriage is marriage. Anyone who is honest with themselves instinctively knows this simple truth. The purpose of marriage is to provide a stable, loving, and orderly environment for the procreation of the human race. Involved in that sexual relationship of husband and wife is not only child bearing. There is also the result of sexual pleasure between the husband and wife that brings them close in their relationship, promoting commitment and stability. Sexual fulfillment between a husband and wife is an important part of the loving environment established in the home. Marriage is the institution that is recognized in every culture. This attempt to redefine marriage as any relationship between any adults is a direct attack on the basic foundation of society. To define marriage as simply being any people in a loving committed relationship is to redefine it. Why not then have three people married? Or twenty people married to each other? Why not allow brothers and sisters to marry? Why not brother and brother, or sister and sister? Why not open marriage up to any combination? Who is to say that any combination is wrong if the homosexual, liberal agenda has its logic embraced? As years go by, with the redefinition of marriage, it will not stop sliding down the slippery slope. Marriage itself will not exist anymore as the sacred union that God instituted, as recorded in the book of Genesis, supported by thousands of year's experience. The arguments that are being made by homosexuals can be used to argue any combination. We have a tendency as humans to believe that things we think are totally absurd will never happen. Over and over again we have seen insane things being embraced that forty years ago one would never think could happen. Would we have believed forty years ago that there would even be one politician in America that would have supported homosexual marriage?

The Obvious

We know that marriage is the unique relationship of a man and a woman. The component of procreation and child rearing is the essential center of marriage. The human body clearly is made to procreate. At the risk of being basic I must simply say: part a) male, goes to part b) female. For those who cannot understand the design of the male and female sexual organs I would suggest that they read a simple anatomy textbook. Now clearly everyone understands what I just described. So what is really at the center of this desire to redefine marriage? After forty years of hearing the liberal establishment rail against the Judeo-Christian heritage of this nation, I can only come to one conclusion. That conclusion is that those who kick and fight against traditional family values have a disdain in their hearts for God's truth as clearly shown in the Bible. At the core of our nation is the foundation of Judeo-Christian principles. Those principles are founded on biblical teaching. That is simply unacceptable to those of the liberal establishment. The psychobabble social engineers profess to be wise and instead have been proven to be fools.

When people such as myself dare to speak this simple truth, we are railed against. We are called bigots, intolerant, hateful, and sometimes much worse.[3] It now has become unacceptable to even disagree with the homosexual political powers. It has now become unacceptable to believe that homosexual behavior is sinful. That is how they have been so effective in silencing the traditional views of America. Many have been convinced that they will be looked at as intolerant and bigoted, so they are afraid to speak what they know to be true. On a political level, they have been very effective in silencing the majority. The power of the liberal establishment is indeed strong in our falling culture. What a wonder it is that no matter how far we fall into social problems in the home, no matter how those social problems lead to decay in our society, no matter how strong truth looks us in the face, the social engineers will not concede the errors of their vain philosophies.

Marriage, clearly defined as one man and one woman, is the unit that has been proven for thousands of years to be the stability factor for society. Why is it that people will fight for what has been proven to be a failure? Why is it that truth is irrelevant to so many social liberals? Why is it that they will not concede what every study has shown? The reason is hatred for Judeo-Christian principles and plain old-fashioned pride. They refuse to admit their failure because to do so would be to admit that all they have put their trust in is a lie.

Illogical Arguments

I must answer one of the main points that the

homosexual population uses to defend their position. They say: "Jesus never mentions homosexuality, so he had no problem with it". This is a lie that has been said over and over. Let me now correct the lie. In the gospel of Mark, chapter ten, verses six through eight, the words of Jesus Christ are recorded as follows: "But at the beginning of creation God made them male and female, for this reason a man shall leave his father and mother and be joined to his wife, and the two shall become one flesh, so they are no longer two but have become one."[4] Jesus here clearly teaches that God created man to be with woman from the beginning of creation. It should also be said that the reasoning of their argument would be illogical even if Jesus did not give a clear definition of marriage. Their illogical argument is that one must mention something in order to be against it, and it must be assumed that the person who did not mention that something must be in favor of what they did not mention. There are a number of things that Jesus did not mention. For example, Jesus never spoke against men and dogs being married. Are we now to believe that Jesus was in favor of that? Using their argument, the answer would be yes. That is how insane their argument is. If a person is not interested in what Jesus had to say about marriage, they can reject what he said, but the misrepresentation of the clear teaching of Jesus on this matter is ignorance at best, or purposeful misrepresentation at worse.

The Small Minority is Forcing the Majority

In conclusion, I must say that we as a society must not allow two percent of the population to take over the ninety-eight percent. No issue is more important to our society. We have already embraced the erosion of marriage in our society with horrible consequences. The social problems that our lack of commitment to marriage has caused is heart breaking. Such demonstrated social problems should have already proven to the liberal elitists the error of their secular thinking. Still they will not concede, and fight on with total commitment to their cause of destruction. Like wolves in sheep's clothing they use words like "loving" and "committed". There is seemingly no end to their influence. TV programs now accept and even glorify the homosexual life as more than normal. In many ways it is portrayed as enlightened. Children's books have been written to influence the most innocent among us.[5] A school in New York City has been established for "gay, lesbian, and "trans-gendered" students. Even in the major denomination that is the Episcopal Church, there has been the ordination of a practicing homosexual man into the office of bishop. This absurd ceremony took place with the new "bishop" standing next to his boyfriend. There never has been, there is not now, and there never will be any biblical support for such an attack on the foundation of God's established institution of marriage. No institution is more important then the Judeo-Christian family to our American dream. Without the family being embraced by society, and supported by public policy, we shall cease to be the great nation that we once were. I pray we come back to this simple truth. The bedrock of our child rearing, economy, freedom, stability, and security is found in the Judeo-Christian family.

United States Sovereignty

The issue of sovereignty and independence as a nation has been debated much over the last 40 years. Some feel that the United States of America should bow its will to that of the community of nations.[1] Some feel that the United States of America should look out for its own interests first and not bow to any other nation's interests over its own.

The diplomatic community is ever trying to unite our common interests. There are forums, conferences, studies, and a whole host of diplomatic endeavors that try to unite the world. When President Bush proclaimed on many occasions in the year 2003 that "the United States does not have to get anyone's permission to defend itself," the globalists were deeply offended. Cries of "unilateralism" were constantly spoken in the media. Those who believe that the United States of America must not act on any self-interest without the approval of our "allies" were horrified. The fact that an American president, who proclaims a belief in Christ, and who proclaims himself to be conservative, would "go it alone" was unacceptable to the leftist elite.[2] Even though over 30 nations were behind our efforts in the Iraq war, it did not matter because we did not bow to the almighty United Nations, and it's "security council."

The False Vision

The vision of a one-world government is something the elitists have hoped for, for many years. They feel that unity among nations would bring peace and prosperity. There would be less and less wars, and eventually wars would cease because of the unity of the human race. Oh, what a great and grand vision. Can you imagine peace in the world, an end to hunger, no more strife and discontentment, and of course a great centralized world power that keeps us all safe and secure? You can imagine it all you want, but it will never happen, that all mankind will live in real peace in this present world that we all live in. This utopian world society is nothing more than a naive look at the nature of human beings. The belief that all people are born basically good and are only influenced to do bad when put in a bad environment- clearly that is an absurd philosophy. History proves that mankind is capable of the most hideous acts of evil, and even those who came from good life situations have in history been consumed with jealousy, rage, selfishness, murder, and the full gambit of evil behavior. Historical facts indicate the clear ability of mankind to do all manner of evil. If people were basically good, there would be little need of a police force, or an army to defend the nation, little need for jails, and other correction programs. It is the height of naiveté to believe that mankind is basically good. Let me remind you that there is no need to teach a child how to do wrong. They know how to be selfish, lie, cheat, and steal instinctively. Children must be taught to do right because as Jesus taught us, we are all in need of salvation because of our inherent sinful state.

The power of the globalization philosophy must not be underestimated, and cannot be overstated.[3] It is a powerful force that now has the backing of the world elite, and awesome technology. That technology is so amazing that it makes the biblical prophecies' fulfillment of one centralized power government not only possible but also likely. The polarization of the American society on just about every major issue is intense. This one is no exception. We are locked in an intense battle of philosophy. Technology is something that can be used for great good, however in the case of globalization it is being used to further an agenda.

Technology is incredibly advanced now in the two areas that matter most: transportation and communication. The ability to move people and product is nothing short of amazing. Perhaps what is even more amazing is the ability to communicate in real time with the other side of the world. Who would have believed in the year 1900 that one could sit down at a desk in America and communicate through instant messaging with someone else in India? Who would have believed that a machine would be invented that could calculate the most intense mathematical problems almost instantaneously? Who would have thought that money could be transferred by the billions each day across nations around the globe? Those who doubted the ability to see the biblical prophecies fulfilled about a one-world government doubted because it was impossible before the information age. Now we see clearly that it has become very possible to control all finance in the world in a centralized manner. The age of cash is diminishing. More people today use credit and debit cards. There is also what is known as smart cards. These cards make it possible to eventually do all one's business electronically. The power of the computer chip is ever increasing. The power of computer centralization is ever expanding.

We are headed for a cashless society. A cashless society gives the ability to have every transaction monitored or at least investigated. There have been various treaties that have set up alliances. The North American Free Trade Agreement is a good example. The effort to have more financial interdependence should be obvious to anyone who looks. Those of us who point this out are dismissed as "conspiracy nuts." The power of financial interdependence among nations is the power to erode sovereignty. As we become more dependent on financial alignments, we lose our ability to make decisions that are in our own nation's long-term interests. We lose our ability to remain a nation with specific Judeo-Christian, constitutional principles. Companies become less American and more multi-national in thinking.

Along with financial interdependence there has also been a movement over the last 20 years or so to what is known as "multiculturalism". This is the belief that there is no superior culture. The belief is that every culture should be respected and embraced.[4] (That is, every culture except classic

American Judeo-Christian culture) The preachers of the multicultural agenda tell us "diversity has made our nation great." They teach that diversity is the main principle of our nation's founding. They point to the great immigration movements of the late 1800's and early 1900's as proof of diversity being the strength of America. Because they push this notion, those on the left try to force our culture to accept all philosophy as being right. Because they believe in relativism, they feel that America must not be absolute in its thinking about our true founding principles.

Diversity or Liberty?

What really made this country great? Was it diversity? Was it relativism? Was it a belief that all culture is on the same level? The answer to these questions is clear. Diversity had nothing to do with our greatness! Have we had diverse people in our country? Yes, we have. Have there been diverse opinions about policy? Yes, there have. Having said that, it is clear that we as a nation had a general consensus concerning our underlying principles. It was in the context of the underlying principles that we had diverse opinions. America was not a place people came to for the purpose of multiculture;

America was a place people came to for freedom under the American constitutional principles. The American society melted into its own culture with constitutional, Judeo-Christian principles as its basis. I submit to you that diversity did not make us great, American liberty that was restrained by Judeo-Christian moral principle is what made us great! Our history is a history of liberation from tyranny. Even in our own country we came to grips with tyranny and freed the slaves. We made it possible for minorities to vote as well. Around the world we have fought with precious blood to free people from bad cultures. We saved the free world from the bad Nazi culture of Hitler's Germany. We fought against the bad culture of Stalin's Soviet Union. The tyrannical culture of Marxist philosophy is as bad as it gets. We fought against the horrific actions of the communist culture in North Korea that was interested in expanding its culture south.

We see throughout history that there have been, and are now many bad cultures. Such cultures include the Taliban in Afghanistan, who have treated women so badly that they were whipped in the streets if not dressed like the Taliban leaders thought they should. These women were not permitted to get any education and could not leave their homes without a chaperone. That is a culture that is opposed to American principles of liberty, and clearly a bad culture! The fact is that many cultures are simply evil. Not all cultures are equal in their worth. The Taliban Muslim culture of Afghanistan was clearly not on par with American culture.

The multicultural crowd is unwilling to admit that America has been great because of its basis in Judeo-Christian principles. They are unwilling to admit that America saved the world from tyrannical domination. It seems that there are many America haters in this country. They are the ones who always blame America for everything. They seem to place the opinions of other country's leaders above our own elected leaders. They worry about what countries like France think. They put great stock in how world leaders, that American citizens have not elected, in the United Nations think. We hear those on the left complain about our nation on a regular basis. I think there are things that need to change in America. The difference, however, is that I feel that the nation must go back to its roots in order to bring about a continued moral and financial future with liberty and justice for all. We have left our understanding of the Declaration of Independence, and have replaced it with multicultural force-feeding by the politically correct liberals. Those America haters are haters of the foundational sovereign principles that America is founded on. Discussion of policy is the American way, however the discussion of the left is an assault on the very foundation of American society.

United Nations: Freedom's Enemy

We have been slowly allowing our sovereignty to erode by giving in to world powers. The United Nations, the World Court, and the World Trade Organization have all been used to subvert our national sovereignty. Add to this the International Monetary Fund and you have a recipe for central-ized tyranny. The United Nations has been trying to regulate by treaty global gun control. They have been trying to regulate family structure and the rights of parents to raise their children in their faith. The United Nations has put into place an agreement that it calls "world heritage sites." These sites are to be kept protected from development or changes.[5] This was agreed to under President Clinton's administration and has placed nearly seventy-five million acres off limits, and under the control of the United Nations. This is an example of the loss of American sovereignty to a world un-elected body of elitists. What right does the United Nations have to usurp authority over the Constitution of the United States of America? Treaties are not to be made that clearly violate the Constitution of this great land. The United Nations has proven itself to be corrupt. During the twelve years of sanctions against Iraq, there was what is known as the "oil for food program." This allowed the government of Iraq to use its oil resources for the purchase of food and medicine for its people. After America liberated Iraq from its brutal dictator, many documents were found that exposed the corruption of United Nations officials who received money from the dictator to look the other way. There were also politicians in countries opposed to America that were receiving money to buy their opposition to our desire to free Iraq from Saddam's grip of tyranny and terrorism. The United Nations is filled with an abundance of un-elected tyrants who sit on various committees. Take for example the Committee for Human Rights in the United Nations. In the year 2004, it was none other than the nation of Libya that was chairing the committee on human rights. That is like asking a wolf to look after the herd of sheep! Libya is one of the most tyrannical violators of basic human rights there is.

The power of globalization and technology, and the erosion of the basic principles America once held dear, is contributing to the loss of our sovereignty. For years the elite have been pushing the notion that we are a "global community." We have heard the phrase "new world order" used for over a decade now. There are those who really believe that centralized power under the United Nations will bring about the peace and order in the world that has eluded us for so long. This grand idea of the power of mankind to fix the problems of the world with the human intellect has motivated the globalist elite. It is the classic delusion that has fooled the masses for centuries: the idea that someone or some central power will look out for the best interests of the people. History (i.e. the Soviet Union) teaches us better; absolute centralized power corrupts absolutely. It is an undeniable fact of history.

This is the reason for the founding of this great nation. Our founding fathers realized that history was filled with tyrants who held power with an iron grip. We established a certain set of absolute principles that set us apart from any nations of the past or present. This Judeo-Christian base of principles made us so unique, that there has been explosive prosperity and freedom like no other nation in the world. The erosion of our sovereignty threatens our very existence as a nation anchored to our founding principles. Multiculturalists are not in favor of elevating our traditional national identity as something for the world to strive for. Multiculturalists are intent on watering our principles down, and having all cultures be seen as equal in value.

No National Border

One of the ways that the multiculturalists see to bring about their agenda is immigration policy. It is clear that the left will not allow any discussion that attempts to change the status quo of American immigration policy. If anyone dares to say that we should protect our borders, then the racist label is used against them. Immigration is one of the interesting blessings of our history. We have had many immigrants, and without a doubt the benefit has been powerful. Many immigrants fought in wars to defend this nation. Many have contributed to areas of math and science. There is clear historical data that shows how immigration has strengthened America.

What is the problem with current immigration? The problem is assimilation. I am not against immigration that makes sense as in our past immigration policy, however there must be the ability to assimilate immigrants into the American principles. We now have illegal immigration occurring at an alarming rate. Millions of people are coming in illegally every year. This is threatening our sovereignty. We must have controlled immigration so we do not lose our set principles. In times past, immigrants came here for a better life and to become American. They were mostly interested in becoming citizens, not just residents. To learn the American constitutional principles is essential in assimilating immigrants into America. There was in times past an assimilation process to the American principles. America was a melting pot of many sub-cultures into the main Judeo-Christian principled culture. Although people spoke their native languages, the society promoted immigrants learning how to speak English so that they could better assimilate. Public policy encouraged immigrants to become American. This greatly contributed to strengthening our sovereignty. Today the multiculturalists do not want us to protect our borders, or our sovereignty. They want us to be in the "community of nations." In their eyes it is arrogant for us to believe that our way of life is superior to any other nation. It is the goal of the left to have totally open borders, and a complete erosion of our

Judeo-Christian foundation.

The left is against us having our common language official. They are against any "unilateral" decisions by our nation. They want us to always consult the United Nations first. They want us to be under the control of a bunch of un-elected, corrupt internationalists. Our Constitution is our Constitution. We are under the rules and God-given protection of our Constitution, not some United Nations charter, or a bunch of anti-freedom, tyrannical thought police found in a fancy building, with lofty titles. The United Nations is an enemy to our sovereignty; it is an institution that seeks to usurp authority over our heritage and our self-determination as a people. They waste our money and do nothing to support our way of life.

United Nations: Clear and Present Danger

The United Nations is a clear and present danger to our way of life. It is a corrupt institution of waste and fraud, and a threat to our sovereignty. There is an effort in the anti-American United Nations to erode the rights of parents. In fact, acting UNICEF director Dr. Richard Jolley at the 1995 UN Social Summit in Copenhagen said: "The state is the guardian of the law. Who but the state can enforce the law and protect the rights of individuals, including children?" At a 2001 convention on Children at UN headquarters, during a video presentation, a Salvadoran youngster declared: "Parents are the principal violators of our rights!" Let's look at a few of the "articles" of the convention.

Article 13 of the Convention would permit a national government to censor a child's access to "anti-government" websites, yet authorize action against a parent refusing to let a youngster download cyber-porn.

Article 14 asserts that the child's "freedom of thought, conscience and religion" must be recognized, which, as applied in the home, has troubling implications for parents desiring to pass their religious convictions on to their young.

Article 19 supposedly protects children from "all forms of physical or mental violence, injury or abuse." Who defines "mental violence?" What about spanking? Well UNICEF official Dr. Jolley was asked about whether the Convention forbids spanking. He replied as follows: "There are some people, I think, that want to maintain the right of being able to beat their children, which the Convention discourages."

United Nations Secretary General Kofi Annan's

style of childrearing is seen very clearly in the "oil for food" scandal. His son, Kojo Annan, is up to his ears in the scandal. Annan's son Kojo is a consultant for Cotecna Inspection SA, a Swiss-based company that won the UN contract to inspect all oil for food shipments into Iraq. Is that not interesting? His son works for the company that was to do inspections. That is a clear conflict of interest!

Liberal Media- The United Nation's Tool

What about the way the liberals protect the United Nations? We all know about the abuse in Iraq of a few prisoners (relatively mild in comparison to what has been done to our soldiers in P.O.W. camps). This was reported and reported, over and over. Interestingly, there is documented horrific abuse under the authority of the United Nations that gets little attention. Human Rights Watch reports as follows:

Human Rights Watch has documented several cases of sexual violence by peacekeepers with the United Nations Mission in Sierra Leone (UNAMSIL), including the rape of a twelve-year-old girl in Bo by a soldier of the Guinean contingent and

the gang rape of a woman by two Ukrainian soldiers near Kenema. There appears to be reluctance on the part of UNAMSIL to investigate and take disciplinary measures against the perpetrators. Reports of rape by peacekeepers with the Economic Community of West African States Monitoring Group (ECOMOG), the majority of whom were Nigerian, deployed at an earlier stage in the war, were rare. Both ECOMOG and UNAMSIL peacekeepers have sexually exploited women, including the solicitation of child prostitutes, whilst deployed in Sierra Leone.

Why is this not front-page news? Should this not be reported even more than the relatively mild abuses by a few American soldier/prison guards? It may be that this story gets traction because the abuse is so egregious but at this point not much is being said, compared to the daily barrage of anti-American reporting concerning the Iraq prison scandal. The liberal media is not out there digging into United Nation's corruption stories hardly at all. If the above report accused the American military of these atrocities, would there be any doubt about how fiercely the liberals would report this? No doubt at all! There are many people, both foreign and domestic, that are in favor of centralized power in the United Nations. Some out of pure ignorance, and some out of desire to destroy the sovereignty of America, and other free nations.

Our founding fathers warned us about being entangled with centralized power, and they understood the principles of liberty. If one honestly studies the philosophy of this nation's founders, it would be impossible to conclude that they would in any way join the United Nations. Just consider the following quotes:

"Every nation has a right to govern itself internally under what forms it pleases, and to change these forms at its own will; and externally to transact business with other nations through whatever organ it chooses, whether that be a King, Convention, Assembly, Committee, President, or whatever it be. The only thing essential is, the will of the nation."

–Thomas Jefferson to Thomas Pinckney, 1792, ME 9:7

"Governments are instituted among men, deriving their just powers from the consent of the governed."
–Thomas Jefferson, Declaration of Independence, 1776, ME 1:29, Papers 1:429

"These are the times that try men's souls. The summer soldier and the sunshine patriot will, in this crisis, shrink from the service of their country; but he that stands it *now*, deserves the love and thanks of man and woman. Tyranny, like hell, is not easily conquered; yet we have this consolation with us, that the harder the conflict, the more glorious the triumph."
–The American Crisis, Thomas Paine

"We fight not to enslave, but to set a country free, and to make room upon the earth for honest men to live in."
–The American Crisis, Thomas Paine

"Not a place upon earth might be so happy as America. Her situation is remote from all the wrangling world, and she has

nothing to do but to trade with them."
–The American Crisis, Thomas Paine

"Arbitrary power is most easily established on the ruins of liberty abused to licentiousness." –George Washington

"But a Constitution of Government once changed from Freedom, can never be restored. Liberty, once lost, is lost forever."
–John Adams, letter to Abigail Adams,
July 17, 1775

"Children should be educated and instructed in the principles of freedom."
–John Adams,
Defense of the Constitutions, 1787

We Must Stand Against

The United Nations, the multiculturalists, the socialists, and all the other anti-American forces in the world must be resisted. Free trade, (fair, not tilted in favor of other nations) working with real allies, and other traditional relations of diplomacy are fine, but we must resist the attack on our sovereignty. The President takes an oath of office. In that oath he promises to "defend the Constitution of the United States of America from all enemies both foreign, and domestic." Globalists, socialists, multi-culturalists, and every other force that centralizes power are enemies of the Constitution. Our modern presidents of both political parties have failed us miserably. Those who are domestic enemies of the Constitution must be resisted. The President and Congress are charged with the responsibility of defending the Constitution, and on all counts of that responsibility they have failed because of political correctness pressure. Our founders were principled statesmen. Our leaders of the past 40 years, with the exception of President Reagan, have chosen short-term gain over long-term freedom and prosperity. President George W. Bush has shown some defense of our sovereignty, but has refused to defend our borders. It is my hope that we as a nation once again grasp the principles that separate us from the tyrants of the world. We must regain our national and constitutional sovereignty. The alternative is world-centralized tyranny.

What About Tax Policy?

One of the most powerful topics in any society is the topic of taxation. It is so powerful an issue, not because of the fact that people simply do not like to pay taxes, but rather because of the implications of a society's tax policy. What do I mean by "implications"? Let me explain.

Tax policy has a direct impact on not only the individual taxpayer, but also on the family, community, nation, and even the world. The worldview of a society clearly is shown by the way it collects taxes. It is also shown by whom it taxes most. Remember, one of the issues America fought the revolution over was the issue of taxation without representation. It should be said that taxes are not the problem but rather one of the symptoms of a greater worldview problem.

Who Provides?

The real issue can be summed up in a question: Should the government be the main provider of benefits to the society or should the private sector?

That is the main question. If one believes the government should be the main provider of benefits then that person has a clear leaning toward socialism at best, or communism at worst. Now in a perfect world that deigns the biblical understanding of mankind's sinful nature, perhaps communism may have worked. If everyone is at the same level of intelligence, cared the same for the so-called "greater good" of others, and worked exactly as hard as the next to share everything exactly, maybe then communism would work. It is clear though that people are not the same. People have differing skills and motivation. The individual person is motivated by reward for work, and incentive to improve and increase productivity. Communism is the ultimate centralization of power and denial of human nature. It is the silly notion that all will be equal in effort and productivity. In a communist society all are supposed to be equal. The problem is that some are more "equal" than others. The elitists in the communist governments do not share their nice homes with the public. They do not have to wait in lines for a piece of bread. Communism is tyranny! It has never, and will never work because it is based on completely false philosophy. The biblical worldview clearly takes into consideration the power of incentive and motivation. Socialism assumes that government is somehow pure in its intentions to redistribute wealth. Socialism assumes that somehow government will protect the individual better than the private sector. This is a trust that has been proven over and over to be not only false, but also in many cases deadly!

To Control or Free?

Taxes are the way a government either controls or frees its people. If a nation, such as America used to be, taxes its citizens less, it therefore depends on private sector growth along with private charitable organizations to provide opportunity.[1] That nation is displaying a worldview that understands that centralized power is corrupting. That society is clearly influenced by an understanding that decentralized government is the best protection from tyranny. That nation only taxes for the essential protection of the nation's basic needs. Representational government then acts to serve and protect because it is not as powerful as the private individual who gathers in the biblical worldview and votes. Having said that, a nation that taxes its productive citizens more that its non-productive citizens only works against the upward mobility of all its citizens. The notion that a productive citizen should be penalized for productivity is not only counter productive to all people, it's just plain stupidity.

Clear Manipulation

Why then is it, that after the failure of communism in the Soviet Union, the clear failure of socialism in Europe, and the clear successful history of this great nation of America, people cannot see that the way to prosperity is low taxes, limited government, and decentralized power? At the risk of being referred to as some kind of conspiracy theorist, I must say there is a conspiracy of sorts. The conspiracy is not, in my view, a group of people in a back room charting the purposeful destruction of our way of life. More likely is the case that the erosion of the Judeo-Christian worldview, along with its results, has caused a snowball effect. The more we go away from our founding, the faster we go away from it. It is exponential in its progress. So now it has become clear in my view that those in power recognize that class warfare is good for them. They not only believe that the government should be the main provider of benefits, they also see the power of using the tax code to manipulate the citizenry.

How is the public manipulated? Well, it is quite simple. The powerful use the power of covetousness. (This is why the 10th Commandment is "Thou shall not covet")[2] What is covetousness? The Hebrew word used there in the 10th Commandment means to desire, or lust after. The implication of that word in its context is that we are not to desire or lust after that which belongs to someone else. The implication is that one must not allow oneself to believe one has a right to that which belongs to someone else. The political elitists use the power of human lust and envy to communicate that those who earn more must be looked upon with suspicion because they must be doing something wrong to be better off than you. The liberals put forth the false notion that we, the powerful leaders in government, are the ones you can trust to protect you against the evil "rich" people. They convey a message that clearly says the private sector is inherently not to be trusted, and the public sector is naturally the sector that can be trusted. So the rich get taxed more, the middle class gets taxed less, and the poor get taxed the least.

On the surface that may sound fair. Why shouldn't the rich pay more? Why should the poor pay anything? The answer is that all should pay taxes that are limited to the least amount possible to keep the nation safe in its duty as defined by the Constitution. If everyone pays, everyone will be concerned about the raising of taxes and therefore will be involved in the political process to keep government from being out of control. As long as people feel that someone else is paying the bill, human nature is to not be as concerned with the bill. Human nature is such that penalization of effort leads to less effort. If we want prosperity, we must allow people who are willing to work hard and take risks to prosper, thereby creating opportunity for those in society that may not be quite as ambitious and/or gifted in the area of creating wealth.

No Clue

The American people as a whole are out of touch with what taxes do. The American people are completely confused by a tax code that no one understands. The IRS itself cannot even understand the code. I had a friend of mine say to me one day when he got his tax return: "I got my tax return back, this is the time when I really love my government." I was blown away by his statement. He was so out of touch with tax reality, that he did not even realize it is his own money! Further more, they had been holding his money interest-free. So in truth, he had even lost money. By using the power of taxes and class warfare, those in political and entrenched power keep themselves in power and confuse the citizenry.

Another way that politicians use tax policy is to manipulate industry. Let me now give you a hypothetical example. A company or industry makes a product that has a large amount of profit and influence in a certain area. The politicians need money to stay in power. The company or industry gives money to their campaign. Then tax policy is changed to reward the company or industry, so indirectly what is happening is an old fashioned pay-off. Only the pay-off is in the form of a tax reduction that leads to a net gain for the contributing company or industry. So with this we see the never-ending merry go round of political manipulation of companies, and company manipulation of politicians. I feel taxes should be low, however I resent the utilization of promises of tax breaks to manipulate industry and the average American. We need to get politics out of tax policy instead of continuing to allow the powers that be to manipulate us. Simply put, we need either a constitutionally capped flat tax or constitutionally capped national sales tax. I prefer the national sales tax.

This would be the fairest tax, and a tax that the political forces would have no ability to use to manipulate industry or citizens.

Look to the Past

History screams out at us concerning the foolishness of trusting government to be productive. Government is the most inefficient way to spend money.[3] Waste has been documented and still there are those who believe that the way to freedom and prosperity is to tax and spend. Money is like water. It flows to the area of least resistance. A society that allows money to be made and kept in the private sector encourages money to flow to create jobs and wealth. A society that penalizes wealth creation is a society that will not prosper. Like water, the money will find another place to flow. Logic dictates that freedom to own property, hold onto one's own finances, and run businesses without excessive government intrusion is great for all citizens.

Total Hypocrisy

Those who want more government point to corporate corruption. In all of the talk in our nation concerning the power of corporations, one must ask the question: what is a corporation? It seems like the anti-capitalism crowd loves to pick on "big corporate America." Clearly those in the corporate world who are crooked must be dealt with and made to suffer the same consequences as the average person would. Having said that, let me remind us all that corporations are made up of people, people at every income level. Most corporations are honestly adding to the well being of America. Yes, there are some corporate leaders who have been found to be crooked. We must however remember that our system is not perfect because no system is. To label all corporate leaders as crooks is how the socialists use class envy to divide us. They use certain phrases like "working families" as if all those who are wealthy did not work for what they have. This implies that a wealthy person does not work. No matter how rich or poor someone is, we simply must punish those who break the law, and reward those who do not break the law!

Having said that, why is it that there is no outcry concerning the biggest crooks there are? Why do we not hear the left screaming about the intense fraud of the Government? We know that the Government is not able to account for billions of dollars.[4] Yes, I said billions. Government workers have been caught using government credit cards for personal use. They have wasted tons of money on retreats to resorts, and clearly no one is ever held accountable. It is a bad joke watching those in Congress lecture crooked corporate leaders. They themselves cook the books to make it look like there is a social security "trust fund." I would have to laugh out loud if it were not for the fact that it is scandalous! How can it be that the worst offenders of the public trust are the government leaders themselves? Could a corporation get away with saying, "We do not know where a billion dollars went"? Would the IRS just say "ok"? Could a corporation get away with making false projections over and over to mislead the stockholders? The government practices that all the time with "we the people" (we are the stock holders of our country). With all the corruption in government with failing schools, wasted money, lost money, political number fixing, and accounting fraud, who do the socialists want to give more power to? You guessed it, the government. With corporations we can hold them accountable. With big government, we cannot do anything. The culture of central power guards it- self. Central power makes laws to cover itself. Government unions make it almost impossible to hold government workers accountable. Why would we want to give more money, more power, more anything, to any institution that has proven itself to be inefficient at best, and downright criminal at worst? The liberal, socialist, anti-capitalism crowd always has the same answer: more government.

Government: Only One Way to Grow

Government itself has only one option concerning its expansion of power. In the private sector, a company must compete for business and expansion of its market share. A private company must function in a lean manner to compete. Inefficiency is the enemy of private expansion of market share and thus the private sector is ever working to increase productivity. On the contrary, government bureaucracy has only one option to grow. It must continue to grab power from the private sector through liberal, political ideology. The more inefficient the government is, the better for the government. They simply use emotional hysteria to motivate an uninformed public that is already dependent upon their particular agency. This emotionalism motivates the uninformed public to allow the government to take over even more of the private sector. Once the government gets a given sector of the population hooked on the crumbs it feeds them, the centralized power creates dependence. This dependence is the only way that the government can possibly expand its power. It is in the best interest of the bureaucracy to be inefficient. Since they know they are never held accountable for their inefficiency, they ask for more tax money, and more power. As insane as it is, the government agencies continue to make a case for more power to fix the problems that they help to create. What is even more insane is the fact that they continue to get what they want. Is there any private company anywhere that could survive if it conducted its business affairs in the same manner as the federal government? The answer is clearly no. A private company would go out of business quickly if it followed the example of the government.

Anyone who has an understanding of the history of socialism or communism should understand the failure of centralized power. As Thomas Jefferson said, "The Government that governs least governs best." Laws are made for the purpose of rewarding those who do good and punishing evil. Our founders would be calling for a revolution if they were taxed as we are. The colossal failure of socialism and communism is clearly documented. Our founders realized this ahead of time. That is why the Tenth Amendment was added. Let me now quote it: "The powers not delegated to the United States by the Constitution, nor prohibited by it to the states, are reserved to the states respectively, or to the people." That means the central power of government must be limited to only what the Constitution says! The rest is for individual states to decide. That means we must take responsibility for our nation, families, neighbors, and ourselves. If not, we are destined to lose the greatness of that which was based on freedom and responsibility. Government is not the answer. Our founding attitude of liberty, God, and having our country live within the restraints of the Tenth Amendment is. If government is limited, government cannot be bought to the extent that it has been bought today. Let freedom ring in the Judeo-Christian base it has been founded on, and let tyranny fall!

Judicial Activism

⬦⇒⇐⬦

W hen I was growing up in school, I learned about the establishment of our government. I learned about a system of checks and balances. This system was put together in a time when most of the world had not even considered such a proposition. The American Revolution was more than just a revolution for America; it was a revolution that sounded around the world in the area of philosophy. A nation "by the people" under clear principles of liberty was a profound idea. This was foreign to those tyrants in the world, and to the elitists in their royal palaces. Could there be a governmental system that looked out for the average person's rights? Could that be? Well yes, it was truly revolutionary in thinking. The Bill of Rights was given for the purpose of protecting the individual citizen. There would be no automatic inherited authority of family members, no royalty, and no laws that leaned in favor of the established powers (in as much as humanly possible). This revolutionary thinking led to the Declaration of Independence, and the

Constitution of the United States of America. These documents were filled with wisdom concerning the understanding of human nature. Human nature is to grab power, and centralize it at the cost of freedom to the average individual. This is why Congress is not allowed to make any law stopping freedom of religion or speech. That primarily was concerning political, religious, and speech of opinion about government officials. These great documents clearly included an understanding of a biblical worldview. "We hold these truths to be self-evident that all men are created with certain inalienable rights." In other words, the acknowledgment of the Creator is an acknowledgment of God.

Checks and Balances

In the system of checks and balances, we have an understanding of the need to keep government in check because of the biblical view that all mankind has a propensity to sin. Sin itself has great power to motivate people in power to abuse their authority. Therefore the need is clear for balance between the three branches of government. Let's look at them: the following is not meant to give an exhaustive explanation of each branch, but rather an overview.

1) The executive branch. The President himself leads the executive branch. He is responsible for foreign policy. He is the chief law negotiator of treaties. He is the commander in chief of the military. He has power to veto legislation, but can be overridden by a two-thirds majority. He also has the power to appoint executive advisors, ambassadors, and judges with advice and consent of the Senate. This along with many other executive powers is outlined in the principles of the Constitution. He is not a king. He is not royalty. He is not given an exclusive right to lead because of any bloodline. He must be elected.[1]

2) The legislative branch. The legislative branch is made up of the Senate and the House of Representatives. This branch has the job of writing legislation. It is made up of elected officials who are to serve the people of this representative republic. They are also not royalty. They also must be elected. Their responsibility is to collect taxes, to coin money, to establish regulations for interstate commerce, etc.[2]

3) The judicial branch. The basic role given by

the Constitution to the courts is to judge in civil and criminal cases. The judicial branch also is given the responsibility to make sure that laws that are made by the legislature are in keeping with the original intent of the Constitution of the United States of America.[3]

Activist Judges

This brings us to the point of this essay. The fact is that judicial activism has taken over our courts. This leftist agenda, along with its liberal social re-engineering goals, has not been propagated by the legislatures fast enough for those who are intent on the destruction of our Judeo-Christian heritage. Because of this, they have sought out liberal judges to bring about their agenda and subvert the representative republican form of government that was established by the Constitution. Al Gore said while running for president, "the Constitution is a living document." Now what he was clearly saying in the context of that speech is that he believed what every other liberal believes. They believe that the Constitution is subject to the liberal thought of the day and not subject to the bedrock founding principles. So a judge may decide whatever he wants based on the prevailing philosophy of his/her personal views. For instance, the Supreme Court decided in 1973 that abortion is a "right to privacy found in the Constitution." Only absurd judicial activist thought can come to that illogical view of the Constitution. There is one way that the Constitution is a living document. That is the amendment process. The amendment process was designed by the framers of the Constitution to be a very tough process. It was designed to be very slow because they did not want the founding principles to be abandoned at a whim. That is the reason that we are not a pure democracy. Democracy is mob rule without any concern for minority view or rights. The Constitution has in it the by- laws for governing the mission statement found in the Declaration of Independence. Our founders realized, as they experienced the abuses of the King of England, that the King did not recognize any "inalienable rights."

They knew that God, who created the heavens and the earth, was the giver of rights, and that no man had a right to take the rights of "life, liberty, and the pursuit of happiness" away. They knew that when governments exercise power in a way that violates those core principles, then government is in

violation of the purpose that God allows governments to be established for. In the past 40 years or
so, the courts have moved more and more away
from the understanding that they are to simply interpret the constitutionality of the laws based on original intent. Now we have courts that tell us the First
Amendment protects pornography, but not political
speech 60 days before an election. They now tell us
that the Second Amendment is not a personal right
of the citizenry even though it is in the Bill of
Rights. The Bill of Rights is about individual rights.
In January of 2004 a judge in Washington D.C.
ruled that the Second Amendment was not a
personal right because Washington D.C. is not a
state. Huh...so the founders did not believe that
those who live in Washington D.C. have inalienable
rights? Washington D.C. citizens are not under the
Constitution's Bill of Rights? That judge is saying
that those citizens of Washington D.C. have no right
of free speech, to be free from unreasonable search
and seizure, or to a speedy trial, etc.? Is he serious?
Is that what he believes? I think not. Clearly that
ridiculous ruling was a way for the judge to subvert
the Second Amendment himself, and thus to subvert
the inalienable rights of the individual citizen. The
core principles of life, liberty, and constitutional

limited government were put in so that there would not be this type of ruling. The Bill of Rights was written to stop this kind of foolish judicial activism. The problem now is that there are many on the bench that seek to subvert the will of the people by overriding the people's representatives in Congress. These judges are activists for their own political and philosophical views at the expense of the constitutional principles this nation was founded on.

Here is the real issue concerning all of this. The Constitution is founded on an understanding of the Judeo-Christian worldview. This is why our first president, George Washington, explains that this system will only work for a religious and moral people. The reason for that is clear. No principle of the Constitution could be upheld without a continuance of the core beliefs of the society. The core belief was in God, and the core belief was in the inalienable rights given by God and not by any man, woman, or government. The country is what it is because of its foundation. If the foundation is eroded, the only thing that can happen is the house will fall. This is why we must get back to our founding and fight against liberalism. The three branches of government must serve again as checks and balances. The only way to assure this is a return to the original intent of the Constitution, and to return to our founding biblical worldview.

Original Intent

Judges must have a strong understanding that their responsibility is to judge according to the truths that are self-evident. They should judge based on the fact that it is the Creator that endows all mankind with inalienable rights. They are not the right-givers! This, in my view, is essential if a judge is to make rulings based on original intent. It must be said that our rejections of the biblical Judeo-Christian worldview as a society have an impact. The impact is seen in our falling away from the Constitution's principles. The more we fall from the Judeo-Christian worldview, the more we fall away from the Constitution, and that means the more danger exists to have our inalienable rights trampled on by centralized power.

Education

Ｈow a nation educates its young people is
very telling of the values of that nation. At
the time of our nation's founding, most kids were
taught at home or in church. The teaching style at
that time was very much motivated by the clear
Judeo-Christian worldview. There is no question
that our nation had a deep faith in the God of the
Bible. The idea that Christmas songs could not be
sung, or that the school could not pray to open the
day, would have been outrageous. The church was
involved in the school in many ways. Mostly the
involvement came in the influence that the Bible
had on the family and individual student. The idea
that a kid could have sworn at the teacher and
gotten away with it (or had excuses made for that
behavior) would have been anathema to any school
philosophy at that time. The problems they dealt
with had little to do with the violence, swearing,
threatening, or any other of the desperate school
problems we have today. The fact is that chewing
gum, passing notes, and the occasional fight in the

school yard between a couple of boys, (who the next day were friends again) were the problems of the day. The family was together. The father led the home. There was work to be done, and clearly defined limits to behavior. This all led to a stable environment that made learning a safe thing to do. There was no worry about getting shot in a cross-fire between rival drug dealers. There was no toleration for back talk, and therefore we had a great education system. There also was no involvement of the federal government. Education was a local matter. No big teachers' unions like the National Education Association to fuel the fire of liberal doctrine, and drive up school costs.

Never Enough Money

Why have we fallen so far from those days? Liberals would make the argument that not enough money is being spent. They say schools are in need of more finances to get a better education. We now spend approximately $10,000 per student in the inner city and still they say it is not enough. It is very interesting to me that we spend so much and we are not even teaching our kids how to read at a basic level. What are the liberals saying? More money! Well I ask this question: If $10,000 is not enough to teach kids how to read at a basic level, how much do the liberals want in order to teach math and science? Will $100,000 be enough? What is the number? The truth is that money is not the issue at all. We throw more and more money every year at education and we continue to lag behind. In the inner city, liberal Democrats have primarily run the schools for the last 40 years. What has happened to the inner city schools under their leadership? We all know what those schools are like. Many teachers will not even allow their own children to attend those schools. Why is it that when we see a failure, we continue to do the same things that made the failure in the first place? The answer is complicated, however I think it can be summed up in a few words: pride, arrogance, and bureaucracy. Those who are in power in the schools want to maintain their power. To admit that they have been wrong for 40 years is something that is too damaging to their own power and psyche. So what do they do? They blame conservatives for wanting to have some sanity in education. They call anyone who wants to stop throwing money at the problem names. They say that conservatives don't care about children, that conservatives are lacking compassion. That we, who believe in conservative principles, really are hard hearted, and only concerned with big business. Well it should occur to them that conservatives also procreate (and we let our children live), and we are very concerned with children. That is why many are home schooling. Those who home school sacrifice much for their children. A possible second income, the money it costs for teaching materials, and a whole lot of time and energy are spent because of the love that these home schooling parents have for their children. At the same time, those who home school still have to pay the excessive taxes for the government school system that has failed.

The Sacred Cow

One mention of changing the status quo and all hell breaks loose in the education establishment. Cries of foul are heard reverberating in the halls of centralized power. Vouchers are a great example of this. Vouchers are one of the greatest ideas in education in the last 100 years. The idea is that the parent is given a voucher that is worth what the government pays per student. The parent then searches out a school of choice for their child.[1] The parent knows best for their child, and if the parent so chooses to put their child in a religious school or non-religious school, or even a government school, that is their choice. This brings a number of benefits to the student. The government schools would no longer be a monopoly. They would not be able to confiscate your money and spend it without any competition. Competition for those dollars would create an environment of excellence. If a school were not performing properly the parent would not allow their child to go to it because they would have another option. That would make bad schools close their doors. It would also make good schools thrive, lifting up all the students with it. The liberals cry out against this. They are totally opposed to school choice. Apparently the liberals want "pro-choice in the killing of unborn babies, but no choice in education of the babies who have lived. This of course makes perfect sense if you understand human nature that is driven with no foundational moral code. They say, "We must protect the public schools." I ask, why should we? I thought the idea was to educate the students, not to protect the government-established monopoly. I thought protection of the children from poor teaching and violence was the objective. Why must we protect the public school system? Why is it the "sacred cow" that cannot be touched? The answer is simple. While the education establishment cries out against conservatives with charges of not caring about our children, the real truth is that liberals themselves have put their own protection of established power and money above the children. They are doing the very thing that they accuse conservatives of. They are afraid to compete with the private sector because they know they will lose. They like the status quo. Competition to them is a threat they will not allow to come about. The liberals rant and rave against the powers of big business when they themselves protect a huge monopoly that serves their own interests. Government education is big business! Any thinking person knows that competition brings more value for the price. It is a law of human nature. If I sell shoes, and you cannot get shoes from anyone else but me, then I can make the shoe any way I want, and charge more than it is worth. If another begins to make shoes and competes with me by being more efficient, the cost goes down. What also happens is the quality goes up because of the choice of who to buy from. If I want to stay in business, I better find a way to make my shoes more cost effective and better in quality. When forced to do so by market forces, the shoe buyer wins with better product, better choices, and better value. This is common sense. Competition brings a better product, plain and simple. The liberals do not want simple common sense answers to problems. If they can make the public believe that things are complicated, they can continue to keep themselves in power. Some things are complicated. However, most problems are just plain simple common sense. A voucher system is a simple answer to a simple problem.

Liberal Circular Reasoning

It is also interesting to note that one of the arguments that the liberal education establishment makes for the failure of education are the problems that kids have at home. I must say that I agree with that statement, however I must also say that the liberal establishment in media, entertainment, and education has been propagating the worldview that has encouraged the very thing that they say is the problem with student home life. The schools are now filled with a liberal agenda, teaching a value system that is politically correct, creating an environment that fuels an attitude that there are no consequences for actions, making excuses for students that behave badly, and classifying students with new "disorders" instead of simply applying discipline. Kids now are told they are A.D.D, A.D.H.D, bipolar, etc. Why these classifications?

They are a great cover for the failure of education. Now we have many kids on mind-altering drugs, given to them because they are so-called "hyperactive." I am not buying it. What is the next excuse the government liberal education establishment will have? One can only imagine. The schools really should exist for one purpose. That purpose is to teach reading, writing, math, science, history, and other pertinent topics. It should not exist to brainwash the students in earth worship, sexual choices, and other liberal slanted information that leaves students believing falsely about conservative ideas. Politically correct secular dogma is the religion of the left in this country, and they are doing everything they can to get the nation's youth to bow to the false god of liberalism. Empowerment comes from competition, and freedom to choose what school a child goes to. Freedom of religion is also upheld. Tax money belongs to the taxpayer, not the government, the government "of the people, for the people, by the people." If you are an atheist you can send your kid to a Godless school. If you are a Christian, you can send your kid to a Christian school, etc. This stops the continued assault against the teachings of the family. The way it is now, the public schools are subverting the religious teachings of a biblical based family. They spew philosophy that is often directly opposed to what a Christian family tries to inculcate to its young members. A choice given to the parents strengthens the family structure and power in the life of the child. Only by speaking out, and making conservative ideas known in the marketplace of ideas, can we hope to change our country back to sanity and common sense.

Abortion

Few issues have divided the country more than the issue of abortion. We hear arguments on both sides concerning who gets to choose if abortion should be allowed or not. Some say it is a constitutional right that a woman has, to do what she will with her own body. This right, they say, must not be infringed upon. Others say that the Constitution grants the right to life, and that no one has the right to kill innocent life, including a woman choosing to terminate her pregnancy.

A Loss of Common Sense

I find the logic that has been used on the pro-abortion side to be extremely flawed. Lets look first at the idea that it is a woman's right to choose. Does a woman have a right to do whatever she wants with "her own body?" We have many laws that limit what a woman or a man can do with their own body. We have drug laws they say it is illegal to take certain controlled substances. The argument is that society has a compelling interest in banning certain substances from personal use. We also have laws against a person taking certain drugs without a prescription from a doctor. The thought is that some things must be limited, because not all people have been trained in the use of certain drugs that may be harmful if taken without proper knowledge. The argument about one's right to do whatever they want with their own body is also challenged by laws that make it illegal to commit suicide. Should one try to commit suicide and fail, the state can at that point make a determination that leads to that person being committed to a hospital. The practice of prostitution is also outlawed in most states even though it has to do with one's own body. The argument that a woman has a blanket right to do whatever she wants, whenever she wants, with her own body is simply not the case. In the landmark case of Roe vs. Wade, the Supreme Court decided that abortion was a constitutional right. They found it was the right to privacy. Why then is it not a right of privacy to do any illegal drugs that a woman may want to do? Why is it not a right to privacy for a woman to take any legal prescription drugs without a prescription? Is it not her own body? Based on the logic of the decision of the court, there should be privacy rights for her to do anything she wants with "her own body." The answer is simple. There is no right given in the Constitution literally or implied that would allow a woman to murder her own child. There is also no ethical way to interpret the founding documents, to lead to the conclusion that our founders considered an unborn baby to be anything but what he/she is: a baby.

This brings us to two questions. First, is abortion dealing with a woman's own body alone? Second, if abortion is also dealing with another body, what implications are found in that from a moral standing? Abortion itself removes any civil or constitutional right of the one being aborted by the decision of his/her mother. The child in the womb has no ability to speak out about the God-given desire to live. The child has no ability to stop the procedure. The child cannot have a hearing before a court of law. There is no due process to argue the case for living. No attorney is provided to argue on behalf of the unborn baby. Some would say that the baby is not really a baby. They would say it is an unviable tissue mass, or not really human yet. Basic science teaches that life begins when the sperm fertilizes the egg. The real question goes back again to worldview. In a society that is increasingly hostile toward the Judeo-Christian biblical worldview, there is no problem making judgments that have no foundation in moral absolutism. In place of moral, and even common sense, we now have a sort of strained logic of relativism that is not logical at all.

Are We the Deciders of What Life Is?

We have now gotten to the place were we decide if a baby is a baby in the womb, by whether or not the mother wants the child. Let me give you an example of what I mean. Not long ago, there was a large media focus on the Peterson case in California. This case involved a pregnant woman disappearing and then found dead along with her unborn child. The District Attorney charged her husband with double homicide.[1] How can this be? Why double homicide? Who says that the child in her womb was human? By charging him with double murder the state is saying that the child was human. If the child was human and had a right to live and not be killed by an outside force, then the state is saying that child had a right to life. Ok, that is clear and pure logic. Let's now examine the pure absurd, convoluted, and illogical thinking that the state then employs concerning abortion. The ridiculous argument by the state is this: if you want the baby in your womb, it is a person. If someone kills you and your baby, they will count it as two persons that have been murdered. If someone tries to kill you but only succeeds in killing your "wanted" baby, we will consider that one person has been murdered. If you on the other hand decide you do not want the baby, we will allow you to go have another person kill your "unwanted" baby, which will not be considered a baby. Instead it will be considered a choice. Common sense cries out against this illogical contradiction.

Now the next illogical thinking concerns the father of the unborn child. Whether the father wants the child or does not want the child, it is irrelevant where the law is concerned. He has zero rights concerning the child. If he wants his child to live, that is too bad. The state has decided that he has no say in anything concerning abortion.[2] However, if the woman decides that the child is a child, and decides the "wanted" baby is to be allowed to live, then the man must pay support for the child who is now considered to be a human being. Is it any wonder why those of us who are pro-life are scratching our heads at the insanity of this convoluted "logic"? This is the logic of our political, judicial, and intellectual minds? This logic is not even close to making any sense at all. How can we look ourselves in the mirror and say that life is life only if we want it to be? How can it be that we have deceived ourselves so much as to make nonsense a guaranteed constitutional right? What about the man's right to his child? Should he not have a say in the child's life? What about the rights of men? Oh I forgot; men are not to have any rights at all concerning their children unless the woman has decided the child is a child in the womb.

No Parental Rights

The liberals further their nonsensical thinking by even saying that a parent should not have the right of consent concerning their own underage daughter having an abortion. The underage child cannot even be given an aspirin at school without parents' consent. However, the traumatic emotional and physical invasive procedure of killing the baby that lives inside her is somehow not the right of the parents to know about? This makes no sense. They are so vehement about their illogical position that if anything even remotely causes society to rethink abortion, they are opposed to it. A force of evil beyond description drives them.

Most people in America are opposed to late-term

abortion.[3] Most feel that it should not be performed after the first trimester. Let's examine that position. I would ask these questions: How about one minute after the first trimester? How about one day after the first trimester? How about one week after? Is it life then and not a week earlier? What about one minute before the end of the first trimester? How about one day before, or one week? Is it not life then, but it's life a week later? We cannot determine these things based on an arbitrary set time. Who do we think we are? There is no scientific way to determine that 30 seconds before the end of the first trimester the baby is not really a baby. Setting a time or making a law that is signed with an official pen does not make that law right, just, scientific, or morally acceptable.

For those who even believe in the hideous practice of partial birth abortion, is it life at the second before the baby is killed, while still attached to the mother? Is life reduced to a technicality? The procedure of birthing the baby partially, killing it, and then saying "technically" if it has not been totally "born" it is not life, is not only a moral failure of the worst degree, it is also a complete throwing away of all logical common sense. At what point do we say it is life? At what point do we say it is murder? If a woman does not want her baby and delivers it herself partially and kills it, then leaves it in a dumpster, is that murder? Is that her choice? We have prosecuted women for leaving their babies to die in dumpsters. Why? Because we have determined that it is murder right after it is born, but not 5 seconds before it is born? Please, I beg those of you who are reading this that are so called "pro-choice" to re-examine your logic. Simply said, life begins at conception and we have no grounds to believe anything else! Therefore we as a society have an obligation to protect the unborn. Only animals kill their young.

Delusional Thinking

Why have we sunk so far? I would say it is not that hard to explain if we understand the nature of fallen mankind. It is a human trait that shows up in history. We start to dehumanize people. The Germans did it in the 1930's and 1940's. They convinced themselves that Jews were not as human as the Aryan race. They justified the killing, plundering, experimentation, and extermination of the Jews by convincing themselves and their society that Jews were subhuman. Once they convinced the majority of the population of this false position, they had no national conscience about being pro-life.

America in its early history of slavery had the same problem. We did not look at the African as human, but more as an animal to be used for the owner's gain. Those who were in favor of slavery had convinced themselves that blacks were subhuman. There was no consideration for their families; they had parts of their families sold to others for slavery. The conscience of the South had been seared concerning this horrible practice. They thought they had a right to choose who would be a slave and who would not. Even some who claimed to be Christian owned slaves, and deceived themselves into believing it was morally acceptable. This is exactly what we have done in the area of abortion. We have convinced ourselves that the baby is not really quite as human as we are. The unborn child is in effect subhuman. If that is the case then we can decide if it lives or dies. Without the clear biblical worldview we will slip further into relativism. We will continue to convince ourselves that wrong is right. We will not be able to right the wrongs as we did concerning slavery without an understanding of God-given moral codes. God help us to understand that a baby is a baby inside the womb and outside the womb. We must regain our moral foundation or worse is yet to come. The slippery slope is continuing with those who advocate euthanasia. In fact, euthanasia is already taking place in America. Now there are those who are arguing that we can choose who is important to society, and who is not. The death culture is thriving. The understanding of the sanctity of life as a gift from God has eroded.

Pro-choice?

There is now a massive attack on all healthcare providers who are against abortion. The liberal "pro-choice" people are quite anti-choice concerning the moral decisions of an individual healthcare provider. The "pro-choice" crowd now wants to force pro-life doctors to perform abortions. There is no end to the insane obsession that the feminists have with killing babies. It is rather disturbing to think that the main issue that feminists rally around is killing babies.

Death Penalty and Abortion

Some make the silly comparison of the death penalty and abortion. They say that if you are pro-life and in favor of capital punishment, you are being hypocritical. This argument is one of the most ridiculous. To say that capital punishment for a convicted murderer, who has taken an innocent life in a premeditated, cold-blooded fashion, is to be compared with killing an innocent baby is twisted logic. Capital punishment is made for those who commit capital crimes. Abortion is the murder of innocent human life that is totally unable to defend itself; this murder is being committed by those who are given the sacred responsibility to protect that life. The fact that the ones who are killing the babies are the very ones that are given the responsibility of protecting them is sickening. In all this, it matters not to the crazed, selfish, man-hating feminists who see abortion as the sacrament of their twisted philosophy.

Impact

What has the impact of abortion been on society? It has had a horrible effect on young people. In the back of their mind they know they have the option of aborting an "unwanted" baby. They have been told it is not really a baby unless it is wanted. This encourages sexual behavior that is without responsibility.

This leads to very difficult emotional scars from promiscuity. It also leads to more sexually transmitted diseases because of the encouragement of more sexual activity. When a woman finds that she is pregnant, and aborts the baby, there are terrible emotional scars after she realizes that she killed her own baby. Post-abortion remorse is a real and serious emotional problem for women when they realize what they have done. I have had many women in my office who were seeking help with the guilt. Thankfully, I have been able to offer them the hope that is found in the forgiveness of Jesus Christ. For many, it takes years to forgive themselves. For many more, they never forgive themselves. This leaves them with a never-ending guilt over the murder of their own child.

The economic impact is also strongly negative. We now have an aging population and not enough younger people to support the needs of the older population. American has killed over forty million innocent babies since 1973: that is over one million, three hundred thousand murdered each year and over one hundred thousand murdered each month! If that does not sicken you than your heart is dead!!!

Let's look at the following scientific medical facts:

1) An unborn baby's heart begins to beat on the 18th day after conception. (Often before the mother even knows she is pregnant)
2) At 43 days after conception, the unborn

baby's brain waves can be read.
3) At 6 weeks after conception the unborn baby moves his arms and legs.
4) At 8 weeks after conception the unborn baby shows clear evidence of the ability to feel pain.
5) At 8 weeks after conception the unborn baby is completely formed.
6) At 8 weeks after conception the unborn baby has his own fingerprints![4]

Planned Parenthood

Let us now consider the largest provider of abortion "services" and propaganda, "Planned Parenthood." This organization was founded by one of the most sick and radical women in the history of this nation. Please consider some of her words. The following quotes are the words of Margaret Sanger, Planned Parenthood's founder.

"The most merciful thing that a family does to one of its infant members is to kill it."

–Margaret Sanger (editor).
The Woman Rebel, Volume I, Number 1.
Reprinted in Woman and the New Race.
New York: Brentanos Publishers, 1922.

"The campaign for birth control is not merely of eugenic value, but is practically identical with the final aims of eugenics."
–Margaret Sanger.
"The Eugenic Value of
Birth Control Propaganda."
Birth Control Review, October 1921, page 5.

"We should hire three or four colored ministers, preferably with social service backgrounds, and with engaging personalities. The most successful educational approach to the Negro is through a religious appeal. We don't want the word to go out that we want to exterminate the Negro population. And the minister is the man who can straighten out that idea if it ever occurs to any of their more rebellious members."
–Margaret Sanger's December 19, 1939 letter to Dr. Clarence Gamble, 255 Adams Street, Milton, Massachusetts. Original source: Sophia Smith Collection, Smith College, North Hampton, Massachusetts. Also described in Linda Gordon's Woman's Body, Woman's Right: A Social History of

Birth Control in America. New York:
Grossman Publishers, 1976.

"Birth control must lead ultimately to a cleaner race."
–Margaret Sanger. Woman,
Morality, and Birth Control.
New York: New York Publishing Company,
1922, Page 12.

"The marriage bed is the most degenerative influence in the social order..."
–Margaret Sanger (editor).
The Woman Rebel, Volume I, Number 1.
Reprinted in Woman and the New Race.
New York: Brentanos Publishers, 1922.

"Eugenics is...the most adequate and thorough avenue to the solution of racial, political and social problems."
–Margaret Sanger.
"The Eugenic Value of
Birth Control Propaganda."
Birth Control Review, October 1921, page 5.

Planned Parenthood is an organization that is

founded on the philosophy of Eugenics. This is the same philosophy that Hitler used to justify killing six million Jews. The founder of Planned Parenthood was a moral degenerate whose stated goal was the elimination of people that she deemed as inferior. This clearly is not based on the founding principles of our Judeo-Christian heritage!

These facts mean nothing to those who refuse to see the logical conclusion of the arguments I have made in this chapter. Our nation's eyes must be opened. The only way to stop this continued murder is for people to wake up and see the injustice just as many did in America concerning slavery. The truth about the pro-abortion propaganda must be told. Hopefully America will repent of this national tragedy.

Psychology

⋆⇒◉⇐⋆

As we have gone away from traditional think-ing over the past 40 years a new "answer" has emerged for many people. That answer comes from a profession that speaks as though it is scien-tific. However, it has no basis in science at all. Now I know many will not agree with me, because our society has bought the big lie that says, "if you have Dr. before your name that must mean you know what you are talking about". Psychology is one of the most inexact "science" professions there is. With no set of moral codes, psychologists counsel on the most important topics of society. Issues like marriage, family life and sexuality are commented on by these counselors with a worldview that is often completely opposed to traditional values.[1] In psychology there is no right and wrong. The only exception to this point is the politically correct values of the day. There is no set of truth, so there-fore there is no judgment made about most behav-iors. The answer that psychology gives is to listen over and over to a person tell their problems, and then charge that person $150.00 per visit. The other wonderful way that psychology deals with problems is to medicate people into submission. The use of mind-altering drugs in this country is staggering. When a kid displays some energetic behavior, the call goes out for drugs to "calm" him down. A.D.D., A.D.H.D, and a host of other "syndromes" are used to label children and cover the failure of parents to discipline their children and the school districts' incompetence.

To Cope or Not to Cope?

How are we supposed to learn how to cope with anything as a society? Instead of learning coping skills, we are medicated. The drug companies love it. We see their ads in which they say, " This may lead to depression", and "That may lead to depression." Then they tell us that taking their drug "may help with that which may lead to depression." What a travesty of public trust. They mess around with brain chemistry under the banner of this "may" help. Secular elitists have been working on replacing pastors with psychologists when it comes to who is looked to as the family counselor. I have experienced this myself. I have been a biblical counselor for many years. From time to time I have counseled people going through the court system, and have been required to give a progress report to the judge. I have had to work with those in the public social work system. The contempt they show for my traditional Judeo-Christian worldview is amazing. They tend to give no respect to my ability to help people based on real moral absolutes. They think it is judgmental to give actual solid moral teaching about behavior or to hold the one being counseled accountable for their actions. It is a clash of worldviews: moral absolutes vs. moral relativism. The traditional family, marriage roles, and child rearing are ridiculed by the psychological community. They come up with new lofty terms to describe just how much smarter they are than the rest of us.

It will surprise many to learn that the last words of Sigmund Freud were: "The meager satisfaction that man can extract from reality leaves him starving." Sigmund Freud, the great guru of psychology, had these as his last words? Is this the man who has influenced psychology so much? Is this the one who is looked upon as having made great strides in helping people? This man's own last words speak volumes as to the failure of psychobabble.

Psychology, The New Religion

Due to the rejection of biblical values in our culture, we now put great value in psychology. Our courts use it, our schools use it, and even many churches rely on psychological mumbo-jumbo. Humanist philosophy is relied on by modern psychology. The humanist Aldus Huxley's last words were: "It is a bit embarrassing to have been concerned with the human problem all one's life and find at the end that one has no more to offer by way of advice than 'try to be a little kinder.' " This is in sharp contrast to the last words of Andrew Jackson, who said: "My dear children, do not grieve for me.... I am my God's. I belong to Him. I go in a short time before you, and I hope and trust to meet you in heaven." Andrew Jackson was a man who believed in Jesus Christ and the Bible. Most of our founding fathers believed in the Bible. This greatly affected our society in a positive way. As I think of this, clear questions come to mind. Were we better off as a society before psychology took hold of our thinking? Are we better off, now that we have rejected biblical thinking and have given our minds over to the thinking of the amoral, relativist, liberal prophets? One can only conclude, from every bit of evidence, that psychology has not helped anywhere near as much as it has caused wrong thinking.

Selfish Philosophy

The question that psychotherapists ask over and over is: "How does that make you feel?" The whole idea is selfish. One cannot always trust one's own "feelings". Sometimes our feelings are just wrong. There is no set standard for advice so therefore truth is relegated to "How do you feel?" Even reality itself is questioned when they say: "That's your reality." Huh? What does that really mean? If "my reality" is that I am a lizard, does that make me a lizard? If my reality believes that two plus two equals seventeen, does that make two plus two equal seventeen? Reality is reality! If a man is stealing money from the bank, it makes no difference what his "reality" is. He is going to jail. (That is, unless some psychologist convinces the judge that the man's childhood experience with his mother, father, grandmother, or maybe even his dog caused him to steal).

In one case I was dealing with a woman who was extremely abrasive in her speaking. She was a domineering type who would lash out, and be very combative with her demeanor and words. I spoke to her about her behavior, and told her she needed to get a hold of her behavior, and to stop making excuses for it. I gave her clear guidelines for proper behavior in communication. She shared this with a social worker who had been working with her dysfunctional family situation for a long time with no change at all. This social worker that was heavily into psychobabble said: "If he wants you to change your way of behaving, he is trying to change your personality. That pastor is being assaultive." I wonder if she would say the same to a wife beater? Would she tell the wife beater not to change his behavior or personality? Would she encourage him to continue to be mean, nasty, and abusive because that is his "personality"? Some people have bad personalities and need to change their thinking. Some people are simply wrong in the way they respond to others no matter what their "reality" is.

I do wish to qualify my comments. I am not saying that there is never a situation when there is a clear problem with the brain. Some people have obvious retardation, or other serious brain problems that may respond to certain medications. What I am speaking about is the philosophy of psychology in general, and more specifically, pop psychology. I am also very concerned with how the drug companies push their products on television, and in other media, with promises of taking care of every emotional problem. The pharmaceutical companies have done great work in many areas of health. However, the pharmaceutical companies are not much better than many drug pushers on the street when it comes to their mind- altering drugs.[2] This junk is given out like candy. It is easy to get any of these from most doctors. Simply saying you are feeling depressed opens the door for receiving these drugs. We tell our kids to "just say no," while we adults take medications that alter our minds instead of dealing with our problems and behaviors. These drugs give us a false understanding of many of our behaviors, and lead us to believe that every bad behavior, every struggle with feelings, and every bad decision is the result of a chemical imbalance. This of course leads us to never take personal responsibility for anything.

Free Speech

One of the unique and revolutionary things about the founding of this great land called America, is the freedom of political and religious speech found in the Constitution. The First Amendment says "Congress shall make no law respecting an establishment of religion, or prohibiting the free exercise thereof; or abridging the freedom of speech or of the press; or the right of the people peaceably to assemble, and to petition the government for redress of grievances." In times past our founding fathers experienced living under tyranny. Freedom to speak out on religious issues or political concerns was not tolerated. History is full of examples of persecution based on religious and political thought.

Even today, in many places around the world, this freedom is not allowed to the citizens of those countries that are tyrannical. In every Islamic state there is tremendous suppression of both religious and political speech. The Islamic worldview is quite different from the Judeo-Christian worldview. They believe in the conversion by the sword, and total obedience to the Islamic worldview; no freedom to speak against it or its political leaders. This is an example as to why our founding principles are unique. They are founded on a clear view of the world that finds its foundation in the moral laws of the Bible. Other cultures that are not founded on the Judeo-Christian worldview are opposed to our way of thinking in America. We have for many years taken for granted our freedoms. In recent years there has been a strong attack on our free speech liberty both religiously, and politically.

IRS Tyranny

Because of Lyndon Johnson in 1954, the IRS began to use its power to limit the political speech of religious organizations. They did this by threatening to take away the tax-exempt status of churches that spoke out in any way that was deemed by the IRS to be political, instead of religious speech. Because of this threat, many pastors are afraid to speak out on topics that may seem political. Recently a church had its tax-exempt status revoked because the church put an ad in the paper saying that President Clinton is an immoral man, and should not be elected.[1] If one is in agreement with this statement or not is irrelevant. The ruling is a clear violation of the First Amendment. We now have a government agency that has the power to regulate religious and political speech under threat of financial persecution. This has a chilling effect on the First Amendment of the Constitution. The First Amendment says nothing about threatening the church with financial consequences for speaking what is clearly religious or political speech. These examples go against two hundred years of free speech tradition in this country. Political correctness began to increase in the years since, until we have what in my view is a bunch of thought police determining what is allowed to be spoken, and what is not.

Thought Police

As a nation we have laws against acting out any thought to break the law. We have laws against conspiracies to commit crime. What we have not had are laws to govern thoughts. It is more than a slippery slope when we attack a person's right to their opinion even when that opinion has not been acted out in such a way as to break an existing law. When we have laws on the books to deal with crime, and then add political or religious thinking that the perpetrator may have had in his/her mind at the time, and then have separate punishment because they think a certain way, that is a problem. On the surface one might say that a person who, for example, uses racial slurs in vandalism should be punished greater because we as a society believe that racism is wrong. However, there is a problem with that thinking. In our country, based on our Constitution, even a person's racist or other unpopular opinions are protected. The rest of us have every right to express our opinion that racism is wrong, but we do not limit that person's right to think what they want. We are not to persecute anyone for their religious or political thoughts, even if the majority finds their position to be unacceptable in practice. We as a representative republic can make our majority position law by voting for the people who agree with the majority view. We cannot however persecute a person for their personal religious or political beliefs. We can only punish a person if they act out on a belief in such a way as to break the law.

Hate speech, or so-called "hate crimes" legislation is an attack on liberty. What happens when society turns and begins to think that your personal religious and political beliefs are hateful? Who will decide what thoughts are acceptable, and what thoughts are not? Who will decide what religious views are "hateful", and what religious views are not? What happens when religious view is opposed to political correctness? Will that automatically be seen as "hate speech"? All of a sudden your thoughts are criminal. Do we want thought police examining our personal religious and political philosophies? I do not think we do, and in fact that type of thinking is against the principles of the First Amendment.

I will make a prediction. If we continue to make laws that punish thinking and ideas, we will eventually lose our right to free speech. Take the homosexual movement for example. Their political agenda is to stop anyone from speaking against their lifestyle. Eventually we will see legislation that outlaws a preacher from preaching on the public airwaves that homosexuality is a sin. That is already labeled in our culture as hate speech. In fact, in Canada that limitation of free speech is already happening. Now, a pastor can be arrested for "hate speech" if he preaches that homosexual behavior is sinful.[2] There are many liberals who want that same law to be legislated here in America. The First Amendment of the Constitution of the United States of America is there for the express purpose of protecting unpopular speech. It is specifically there to protect religious and political speech as it clearly states in its original intent. If the liberal, anti- Constitutional forces in this country had their way now, they would outlaw speech that they deem hateful.

Say What You Will, Think What You Will

I do not like it when people say what I consider to be hateful things about me. I am not happy to hear the names I am called by the "peace-loving" liberals. Having said that, I believe they have a right to think what they want, and to express their thoughts without fear of punishment from government, EVEN IF THEY SAY THAT THEY HATE ME BECAUSE I AM CHRISTIAN. The line is drawn on their actions. They may not do anything to violate my right to be protected by the law. At the point that they step over the line of thought and speech into violating the law, that is when government must punish. I also reserve my right to respond to any attacks that come my way with my free speech.

Political Speech

Recently Congress passed "campaign finance reform". This legislation is a clear violation of the

First Amendment. It limits the political speech for a set time period before an election date. This is an abomination to the American system of religious and political free speech. This indeed is the single worst attack on the First Amendment in the history of this republic. President George W. Bush signed this law. It was challenged, and came before the Supreme Court. The Supreme Court ruled that the law was constitutional. That is a disgrace, and further evidence of the deterioration of our founding constitutional principles. Now for that legally set period before an election date, only the news media may have freedom of speech, and not any other political group concerning a particular candidate. Our founding fathers are turning in their graves over this. By admission, most people in the media are left leaning politically. Most name themselves as Democrats. Most say they vote for Democrats most of the time. This means that the only people who can influence the public in the marketplace of ideas and political thought are people who have one main political view. Can anyone really say that James Madison, Thomas Jefferson, George Washington, John Jay, or any of the founding fathers had this limit of speech written into the Constitution? No one who is honest would say that our founders would have supported such restrictions of political speech.

Supreme Court or Kangaroo Court?

Interestingly, the same Supreme Court decided that certain forms of child pornography are protected by the First Amendment. Huh? That is insanity! Would anyone really believe that our founding fathers wanted child pornography protected and not political speech for a set time before an election? Is that the reason they wrote the First Amendment? No thinking person who understands the intent of the Constitution would believe such nonsense. Because we now live in a postmodern society, the pop culture elitists believe that the Constitution is subject to pop culture's fluid philosophy.

The relativism that governs the elitist mindset rejects any absolute truth. Absolute principles are seen as close-minded views to them. They have forgotten, or should I say rejected, the objective truth found in the Constitution's worldview. Freedom of political and religious speech shall not be "abridged". There is no power to defend our liberty (as defined in the Declaration of Independence) if we do not hold these truths to be self- evident, that all men are endowed by their

Creator with certain inalienable rights: life, liberty, and the pursuit of happiness. Free religious and political speech is essential for the protection of those inalienable rights.

Gun Control

One of the traits of tyranny is to disarm the public so the public will have no power to defend itself against the government. This clearly was in the minds of our founding fathers when they put the second amendment in the Bill of Rights. The right to bear arms is essential to freedom. With an examination of history we can chart the tyranny and clearly relate it to the confiscation of the general public's arms. This confiscation led to a citizenry that was defenseless against any aggressive move of centralized power. Like it or not, the use of force determines power and rule. The ones with arms are able to rule over those who do not have arms.

Germany

Look at Germany in the time that the Nazi party took control. The law on firearms & ammunition was set in place to disarm the public. The earlier laws put into place in 1928 gave clear documentation about who owned firearms because of the registration process.[1] All gun owners were required to get a permit from the police. By the time the Nazi party gained control, it was easy for them to take firearms away from anyone they deemed a threat to their power. This also eliminated the ability of people to acquire firearms to defend themselves as the Nazi party government became more and more tyrannical.

Hitler, on April 1, 1933, proclaimed a boycott of all Jewish owned stores. On April 7, 1933, Jews were banned from serving in any civil service. On April 7, 1933, State government independence was abolished to total centralized power under Hitler. On May 2, 1933, all trade unions were dissolved. On October 4, 1933, Jews were banned from serving as editors of newspapers. A concerted effort was made to disarm all Jews. By the end of 1933, the primary owners of firearms were Nazi party members. The state and the Nazi party were one and the same once Hitler gained total control. There was no debate or discussion of differing opinions on worldview.

No Defense
Once the Jews were unarmed they were at the mercy of the powerful centralized Nazi government. The Nazi party was known for many things,

but mercy was not one of them. And so we all know the outcome of such tyranny: SIX MILLION Jews slaughtered with no ability to fight. Could it be that if the Jews were armed that they could have stop-ped the Holocaust? I don't think we can say for sure, but we can say this: it is very possible that many Jewish people would have been saved. It is also very possible that an internal effort of guerilla-style warfare could have shortened the war itself. One thing that we do know for sure, at the very least there would have been the ability to fight against the murderers and their minions, and that alone, in my view, would have been much better than being led away to die in concentration camps with no ability to try and stop it.

Jay Simkin, Aaron Zelman, and Alan M. Rice of "Jews for the Preservation of Firearms Ownership," have compiled an excellent book called "Lethal Laws." In it they reveal some startling facts about the twentieth century.

1) The Ottoman Turkey Government murdered 1 – 1.5 million Armenian people from 1915 –1917, after the gun control laws of 1866 and 1911 were put in place.

2) Soviet Union governments murdered 20

million anti-Stalinists from 1929 –1953, after the gun control laws of 1929 were put into place.

3) Nazi Germany murdered 13 million Jews, Gypsies, and anti-Nazis from 1933 – 1945, after the gun control laws of 1928 were put in place.

4) China murdered 20 million anti-Communists, and pro-reform groups from 1949 – 1976, after the gun control laws of 1935 and 1957 were put in place.

5) Guatemala murdered 100,000 Mayan Indians from 1960 – 1981, after the gun control laws of 1871 and 1964 were put in place.

6) Uganda murdered 300,000 Christians and political rivals from 1971 – 1979, after the gun control laws of 1955 and 1970 were put in place.

7) Cambodia murdered 1 million educated people from 1975 – 1979, after the gun control laws of 1956 were put in place.

The staggering number of murdered unarmed civilians just from these tyrannical governments alone is approximately 55.9 million people!

History Teaches Need for Guns

One only has to look at the history of gun control to see that the main threat of gun violence comes from governments that have all the power, and all the weapons. We should be much more concerned about gun violence by governments than we are by criminals. Yet, we buy the lie of gun control organizations that never report anything against governments of tyranny. They use emotionalism to convince some in the public and most in the media that guns are evil, that private ownership should not be allowed. Some of them say that only "sporting rifles" should be allowed. This however completely misses the point of the Second Amendment. The Bill of Rights is about the specific rights of the citizens, and not the government. The Second Amendment is clearly there as a means for the "people" to bear arms in defense of liberty. Any other interpretation of the Second Amendment is at best uninformed, and at worst a deliberate attempt to leave the people open to tyranny.

Common Thread

The common thread in the murdering governments I mentioned is centralized power, confiscation of firearms, rise of strong tyranny, and the wholesale murder of those who oppose the tyrannical government's policies. It has been said, "I don't trust a government that does not trust its citizens with arms." That statement rings out loud and clear when one examines history. History is filled with examples of this. Another saying that clearly rings out today is this: "Those who do not understand history are destined to repeat it." This is why Thomas Jefferson said, "The price of freedom is eternal vigilance." There will always be a tyrant trying to take power from the average citizen. There will always be the fight between excessive centralized power that protects itself, and those common citizens who must fight to protect their liberty.

Criminals Obey Laws?

Now, having said all that, let's put aside for the moment the threat of tyranny since we have clearly seen here that history has proved my point, and go to the illogical position that gun control makes us safer in a society. The thought is that by taking guns away from law abiding citizens there will be a reduction in gun violence. In other words, less guns means less gun violence. This is another case of liberal ideas that sound good on the emotional surface, but have no basis in logic. First we must realize that a gun is an object without any ability to make a decision. The gun cannot stand up, walk into a room, and start shooting people. The gun is simply a tool that can be used for evil or good. The gun can be used in hostility or used to defend against hostility. The liberals have the silly notion that a gun law will be followed by criminals who by definition are people who break the laws. Does anyone really believe that a person who is ready to murder someone (which when I last checked was against the law) is going to stop because the law says guns are illegal? That is preposterous thinking. When people who follow the law are made to give up their arms, or are restricted in their right to bear arms, the only people left with arms are those who do not follow the law anyway, and the government. Washington D.C. is a great example of the failure of gun control. The most restrictive gun control is in Washington D.C.[2] The fact is that crime there is rampant: murder, robbery, rape, and violent drug shootings are among the highest in the land. Interestingly, Vermont, New Hampshire, and many other states with little gun control are lower in crime. The fact is that if you disarm honest citizens, you not only leave them defenseless, you also encourage criminals who now know that their chances of being shot by one that they commit crime against is very low. On the other hand, if the criminals know they may be shot they are deterred from crime. This again is common sense. It seems to me that the anti-gun people are ignoring statistical and historical facts. So to sum this up, our founding fathers put the Second Amendment in the Bill of Rights, because it is our right to defend ourselves from all enemies of the Constitution, both foreign and domestic.

Racism

There seems to be a fixation on race that is so militant, that anyone who dares to make suggestion not in keeping with political correctness is labeled a racist. The dreaded label of "racist" is the weapon used to silence any critic of the so-called "leaders" of minorities. I wish to start out my comments by stating that I am sure I will be called the dreaded "R" word because of what I am writing. I however have never been one who is intimidated by lies that people tell about me. I will speak what I know to be true, and my critics may call me whatever they want.

Fixated

Our country seems to be fixated on race more than any other topic. It has gotten to the point where we no longer look at ourselves as Americans. Instead, it seems that we have placed ourselves in racial groups. The Civil Rights Movement started out to right a serious wrong in this country. Discrimination based on one's skin color is not only against our Constitution, it is just simply ridiculous. All people have the right to life, liberty, and the pursuit of happiness! As a pastor, I have ministered to many people of every skin color, and all that matters to me is that Jesus came to save all people. Those who twist the Bible and use it to discriminate against others based on the color of their skin are simply twisted.

We all know about the white supremacist groups that hate blacks and Jews. They call themselves Christians while at the same time they have no understanding of the Bible at all. They must not have read about Jesus who was a Jew. They must not have read about the Ethiopian man that Philip explained the message of Jesus to. They somehow have not discovered that more non-whites than whites practice Christianity. These truly racist groups are simple-minded fools who use the banner of Christianity without any understanding of the substance of it. Although I accept their right to free speech, I also reserve my right to free speech. I will now use that right by saying that the so-called Aryans, white supremacists, KKK and any others like them are sick individuals! They are an embarrassment to any real American.

I am old enough to know that even though I

made myself clear in the previous paragraph, I will still be called the "R" word. The reason is simple. The liberal minority leaders in this country have decided that anyone who is against their illogical ideas must be against their people. Take as an example "affirmative action". This is the notion that giving preferences to black people over whites simply based on the color of one's skin is the way to fix the problems of the past. Companies find themselves hiring people in a quota system so they are not sued for discrimination. This practice itself is illogical. If our moral consensus is that discrimination based on skin color is wrong, than how can it be good to discriminate based on the skin color of whites? Racism is racism, no matter what race is practicing it. The idea is to not allow the discrimination because it is morally wrong. The problem with the idea of affirmative action is that it is based on the idea that two wrongs make a right.

The word "discrimination" brings up many feelings in the emotions of people. The fact is that Martin Luther King made what is in my view one of the greatest comments on how we should make judgments. He said in his well-known speech of August, 28th, 1963 these words: " I have a dream that my four little children will one day live in a nation where they will not be judged by the color of their skin but by the content of their character."[1]

This statement flies in the face of what we see today. The modern civil rights leaders seem to be steeped in the idea that all white people are racist. I understand how the bitterness from past injustice can make one not see clearly at times. However it is completely unfair to blame everyone for what some in the past did.

Reasonable Discrimination

This brings me to the point of discussion concerning the word discrimination in general. Like it or not, there are some clear things that are allowed to be discriminated against. For example, if a private women's organization wants to have a woman as the head of the organization, they have every right to do so. If a black organization wants to have a black person lead their organization, they have the right to do so. Like it or not, in the first example, that is gender discrimination. In the second example, that is racial discrimination. There is no way around that fact. Would we expect a black women's organization, for example, to have a white male as its leader? Of course we would not. The truth is that every day we make decisions that are based on many types of discrimination. We have companies who do not hire people who have a criminal record or who test positive for drug use. All of these are clear and reasonable discriminatory practices. Having said all that, somehow we feel it is discriminatory to judge people's entrance to college based on performance. If not enough blacks get better scores on entrance exams into certain schools, the answer of the affirmative action proponents is to lower the standards. That means there may be a student who happens to be white who is excluded from a limited number of positions based on skin color, even though he may have scored higher. The "everything is racism" crowd thinks that under-performing students or workers should be promoted simply because their skin color is not white. This is discrimination that's based on an illegal and immoral idea.

If we are to be honest about lack of racial representation, we could look at the National Basketball Association. There's a disproportionate amount of blacks in professional basketball as compared to whites. If we take the affirmative action philosophy to heart, we should limit the number of blacks and increase the white players. This would mean that whites are proportionately represented. This of course is absurd. No one would advocate not having the best players, no matter what their race is, in professional basketball. Why then should we lower the standards on much more important careers, such as medical students, based on the color of skin? The most qualified in any profession should be what brings gain, not preference based on skin color.

English? Spanish? Chinese...etc?

Another area of trepidation for the "everything is racist" crowd is the matter of language. This country speaks English as its language. For over 200 years of our history people who came to this country learned how to speak the English language. In recent years we have been encouraging people not to learn the language. With bilingual education, and changing the language in certain government documents, etc, there have been more and more people who have not learned to speak English. Now if one has an argument to make about their position, on the importance of one official language or one hundred languages is really not the point. The real point I would like to make is the position that so many liberals take concerning those who think it is good for our country to have an official language.

The English language is the most obvious choice. Liberals cry racism when anyone advocates English as the official language. What is racist about a country thinking it should be able to communicate with itself? Is it anti-Hispanic to believe that those who come here should learn how to communicate? What is with all these sensitivity police? The question is simple. If we have many languages being spoken in society at businesses, or in government establishments, it will be quite difficult to do business. That's all there is to it. Why the outcry of racism? If there are people who think that it is good to have confusion in the work place and in government, they can argue their position. Do we always have to hear the charge of racism whenever there is a disagreement with people who are not white? Has this not gotten completely out of control? I think it is time to stop the "R" word label from being placed on people who have a different opinion. No one is saying it is against the law to speak another language. They are simply saying that we ought to have a common language that we all understand. Since it is the case that most people speak English, it would make no sense to choose Spanish or any other language. This is not racist at all, this is simply common sense.

Fast Tracking

Companies use this practice in a policy called "fast tracking". A company may have certain rules and requirements for career advancement for its employees. An example would be how long one has been employed, or a certain chain of positions in the company one must go through to be eligible for consideration of management positions. In the "fast tracking" policy, women and minorities are given exemptions from some or most of these requirements in their desire to promote minorities. This means the only ones who cannot "fast track" are white males. Is this what Martin Luther King meant by judging people not by "the color of their skin, but by the content of their character"? The policy of fast tracking is simply discrimination in the work place based on skin color, or gender alone! That is racist and that is sexist!!!

All White People Are Racists?

I think it is unfortunate that slavery is used to portray all white people as racist and inherently evil. The truth is that many races have practiced slavery. It was often black people who sold their fellow blacks to the white slave traders. In the Sudan there is slavery practiced now of black people by black slave owners.[2] We hear almost nothing about it from the black leaders in this country. By contrast, American black leaders protested the system of apartied (with good reason) in South Africa loudly. It seems that the black leaders were more concerned about the South Africa situation because whites were doing the injustice, but not a word is said about injustice practiced by blacks. Injustice is injustice, no matter what the skin color of the perpetrator of the injustice is. The fact is that slavery is simply evil, and morally wrong.

The political agenda of the main black leadership seems to be to use anything to advance liberalism. The liberal black leaders do not give black conservatives the time of day.[3] There are many black people who are trying to speak out with a conservative voice. There have been conservative black judges up for important judicial positions who have been blocked by the black caucus and white liberals in congress. They are blocked because they are not towing the liberal line. What about the black "leaders" like Lewis Farrakhan? He said: "Jews are the gutter religion." Jesse Jackson made his famous "Hymietown" comment about New York being a Jewish town. These racist comments were not a big deal to the other black leaders. Why was there no outcry? Why was there no public rebuke of the racist comments made by these black leaders? All true racism is bad no matter what the color of skin the comment comes from. White racists are not justified by the fact that there are also black racists, and it is also true that black racists are not justified because white racists exist. Wrong is wrong.

Having said all this, it is important to mention that there will always be people who are prejudiced. There will always be people who dislike others based on a myriad of external reasons. To simply focus on every bad thing of the past and live with a victim mentality will never bring success. The answer is to focus on achieving the best that an individual can, and to compete for positions based on merit. The way to success is to look forward and work hard. There are many opportunities in this country. Blaming everything on racism is a sure way to get less productivity. It only leads to a victim mentality. Where there is real and true racism we must confront it. Where there is blame for everything on racism, and discriminatory answers to end discrimination, we must not give in to that illogical idea. It is my hope that the statement, "judge by the content of character and not by the color of one's skin" would come to be how we think of race. It is time to stop unfair practices that wrap themselves in the name of being fair.

Conclusion

⋆⇒◯⇐⋆

I trust as you have read this book, your heart has been open to the truth found in it. It should be clear to the thinking person that our culture has deteriorated because of our slip into liberalism. Our post modern, relativistic, and humanist mindset has had evil consequences. There have always been some sub-cultures in America. There have always been atheists. There has always been evil behavior, and there has always been sin, and sinful consequences. The problem now is that the sub-cultures have risen to the cultural norm, and the true culture of America's founding has become in many ways a sub-culture. As one examines our history, the only logical conclusion that can be reached is that since we have turned our backs on the Judeo-Christian principles of our nation's founding, we have had a tremendous increase in negative consequences. The family structure is decimated. The public education system is a colossal failure. The simple basic manners of decency are almost non-existent in our movies, and other media. Our rights as free Americans are being eroded. We without a doubt are raising generations that have no understanding of our heritage.

I have made logical arguments in all the chapters. I have used hot button topics to express the danger and absurdity of relativism. I have done this all with absolutely no regard for "political correctness." It is clear to me that I will be greatly maligned for speaking the truth without holding back. I know I will be called many awful things, and there will be character assassination against me.

To me it is worth it. I am one who loves this country. It pains me to see it deteriorate into a cesspool of psychobabble, liberal nonsense. I believe that if you think about the facts, and you open your heart, you will see the error of our fall into liberalism. I can only trust that God will open our eyes as a nation before we fall too far, and reap what we have sown.

May God bless this book, and may God continue to bless this nation with his mercy, grace, and truth. May we come back to the foundation that this house called America was built on. Amen, and Amen!

Reverend David M. Berman

Endnotes

Chapter One

    1)   Christian Apologetics & Research, www.carm.org

    2)   The Eightfold Path, Ch'onsa Kim, www.indianest.com

    3)   King James Holy Bible

    4)   *Humanist Manifesto*, 1933, A.H.A.

    5)   Lawton Chiles, May 31, 1996 quote

Chapter Two

    1)   Declaration of Independence, July 4, 1776

    2)   King James Holy Bible

    3)   A.C.L.U.

    4)   Stone v. Graham, November 17, 1980

    5)   Newdow v. U.S. Congress, June 26, 2002

Chapter Three

    1)   Tenets of Naturalism, www.naturalism.org

    2)   *What if Jesus Had Never Been Born?*, Thomas Nelson, Nashville, 1994, Kennedy/Newcomb

    3)   *On the Origin of Species*, 1859, Darwin

Chapter Four

    1)   Barna Research Study, January 12, 2004

Chapter Five

1) As examples: Everybody Loves Raymond, Home Improvement

2) Time Magazine cover story, July 17, 1995

3) www.menweb.org/throop/bash/quotes.html, quotes from famous feminists

4) www.childstats.gov

Chapter Six

1) www.childstats.gov

2) www.gaycity.com/family

3) www.glad.org, www.hatecrimes.org

4) King James Holy Bible

5) *Heather Has Two Mommies*, Other Words Publishing, 1989, Newman

Chapter Seven

1) Strobe Talbot, Dep. Secretary of State/Clinton Admin. Quote from Time magazine, July 20, 1992

2) 2004 Democratic Party Platform

3) Proposal to Create World Peace, submitted by Karen Holmes, principle, World Peace Organization, March 19, 2003, to United States Senator Gordon Smith of Oregon

4) American Psychological Association, policy guideline #6, August 2002

5) www.cr.nps.gov/worldheritage/tentlist.htm, state by state list of "world sites"

Chapter Eight

1) www.vaughns-1-pagers.com/economics/income-tax-infla-tion.htm, chart showing tax increases

2) King James Holy Bible

3) www.heritage.org/Research/Budget/bg1840.cfm, list of ten obvious government wastes

4) U.S. Department of the Treasury, *2003 Financial Report of the United States Government*, pp. 126, March 28, 2005, fms.treas.gov/fr/03frusg.html, unreconciled transactions totaled $3.4 billion in 2004

Chapter Nine

1) Article Two, U.S. Constitution

2) Article One, U.S. Constitution

3) Article Three, U.S. Constitution

Chapter Ten

1) www.schoolchoices.org

Chapter Eleven

1) People of California v. Peterson, Stanislaus County Superior Court, December 1, 2003

2) Stachokus v. Meyers, Pen Supreme Court, August 2, 2002

3) www.Pollreporting.com

4) www.abortionfacts.com, Dr. J.C. Willke

Chapter Twelve

    1)   McKay and Fanning, 1987, 293

    2)   www.addictionbyprescription.com/facts.html, sales figures

Chapter Thirteen

    1)   Church at Pierce Creek, Binghamton, NY

    2)   Canadian Hate Speech Bill #C-250

Chapter Fourteen

    1)   Germany Gun Control Act of 1928

    2)   Washington D.C. enacted a virtual ban on handguns in 1976. Between 1976 and 1991, Washington D.C.'s homicide rate rose 200%, while the U.S. rate rose 12%.

Chapter Fifteen

    1)   Delivered on the steps at the Lincoln Memorial in Washington D.C. on August 28, 1963

    2)   www.sudanupdate.org/REPORTS/Slavery/slave.htm, report of Sudan slavery, Anti-Slavery International

    3)   *How the Left Trashes Black Conservatives*, FrontPageMagazine.com, July 10, 2002, John Perazzo

Biography of
Rev. David M. Berman

Reverend David M. Berman has been in active ministry since 1985. Over the years, he has been responsible for the planting of two successful churches (one as an assistant with another pastor and one on his own). He holds a theology degree from Atlantic Southern Bible College where he graduated with high honors.

Rev. Berman is also a very experienced and effective public speaker. He has spoken at Dartmouth College, the University of Massachusetts, and Keene State College, as well as many pro-family rallies. Of particular interest to Rev. Berman is the area of affecting the culture with Judeo-Christian principles. He has been a guest on many radio and television shows commenting on various social issues. A feature story about his life testimony was shown on Pat Robertson's show "The 700 Club." He served as pastoral advisor to the New Hampshire Christian Coalition.

Rev. Berman is fully ordained as a minister of

the Gospel with the Christian and Missionary Alliance Church, a large denomination with 17,000 churches around the world. He has been married to his wife Brenda for over 20 years, and they have five children.

Printed in the United States
34512LVS00003B/1-66